Shining a Light

Women of Mackay

Dr Kaaren Sephton, PhD

Copyright © 2025 (Dr Kaaren Sephton)
All rights reserved worldwide.

Cover designed by Black Owl Designs of Mackay

No part of the book may be copied or changed in any format, sold, or used in a way other than what is outlined in this book, under any circumstances, without the prior written permission of the publisher.

Inspiring Publishers
P.O. Box 159, Calwell, ACT Australia 2905
Email: publishaspg@gmail.com
http://www.inspiringpublishers.com

A catalogue record for this book is available from the National Library of Australia

National Library of Australia The Prepublication Data Service

Author: Dr Kaaren Sephton
Title: Shining a Light: Women of Mackay
Genre: Non-fiction

Paperback ISBN: 978-1-923250-72-7

Acknowledgements

The Mackay Family History Society (MFHS) staff have provided me with basic summaries of many notable women included in this book. MFHS have given invaluable assistance, providing access to resources and research advice. I need to thank the State Libraries of Queensland, Tasmania, New South Wales, and Victoria. I also need to thank staff at the Mackay Regional Library Service, Greenmount Historic Homestead, James Cook Library – Special Collections; Pioneer Valley Museum, Mackay Museum, and Sarina Museum, Queensland, for providing information about many of these women and for providing access to their collections. A special thank you to the families and friends of these women for providing me with invaluable information.

The National Library of Australia's (NLA) collection has proved invaluable. I wish to thank the NLA staff for their assistance to access those resources. I also want to thank the National Museum of Australia for their support and assistance.

As a former Visiting Fellow at the Centre for Heritage and Museum Studies, Australian National University (ANU), I wish to thank university staff for their support and allowing me access to resources.

Table of Contents

Acknowledgements iii
Introduction 1
Background 26
Biographies 30
Arbuthnot, Margaret (1874–1959) 30
Arrow, Gloria Jean (1941-2021) 35
Atherton, Letitia Jane (1849-1934) 40
Azar, Mary (1876-1957) 44
Barlow, Grace Elizabeth, Matron (1884-1972) 50
Berry, Dr Annie Hayes (Nan) (1912-1998) OBE 55
Cook, Dorothy Berris (1909-1995) 59
Cook, Elizabeth Cormack Ross (1838-1907) 67
Cook, Vida Althaea (1875-1955) 71
Cooke, Jane (1812-1888) 77
Cronin, Amelia (1894-1972) 81
Derrer, Sister Mary Jane (1892-1986) MM 86
Finger, Hilda (1891-1916) 92
Finlay, Mary, Miss (1886-1966) 97
Fudge, Naomi (1864-1946) 101
Glenny, Ethel Victoria Octavia (1878-1962) 106
Insch, Margaret Mitchell (1854-1944) 109
Kemmis, Emily Slatyer (abt.1845-1913) 114
Knezevic, Catherine Ann Stevenson (1957-2022) 118
Koch, Maria Verena (1844-1937) 121

McBurney, Maria Emma (1849-1935) 124
McDonald, Barbara (1869-1901) 128
Marlla, Katie (Kitty) (1860-1944) 132
Marten, Annie Pring (1851-1933) 137
Martin, Elizabeth Watt (1846-1911) 141
Melba, Nellie (1861-1931) Dame GBE 145
Neilsen, Beryl Anne OAM (1941-2023) 152
Ramsamy, Nolear (1917-2021) 157
Ready, Mary (1832-1902) 163
Robinson, Mary Alexander Goodwin (1850-1925) 167
Sam, Mary Ann (1866-1936) 174
Shuttlewood, Norma May, OAM (1925-2023) 179
Struthers, Mary Ellen (Min) (1903-1988) 184
Tanner, Eliza Jane (1866-1935) 187
Trieve, Rowena Evelyn OAM (1931-2018) 191
Wallman, Marilyn Joy (1958-1972) 195
Wood, Hilma Pansy, Miss (1903-1984) 202

Introduction

A chart exhibition was held for Mackay's early settlers in 2012 and 2016 by Mackay Family History Society (MFHS) at the old Town Hall. The Pioneers of Mackay Charts Exhibition was held in October of 2016 at the Old Town Hall in Mackay, Queensland. This was the town hall that had withstood the wind and floods of the 1918 cyclone. A Regional Art Development Fund (RADF) was obtained from Arts Queensland to promote and develop arts, culture and heritage in the Mackay region by the MFHS. The society received a Gold Award at the 2021 Heritage Festival.

> The volunteers of the Mackay Family History Society delivered two informative and immersive community exhibitions in 2021. The exhibitions displayed family chart information on the early settlers of Mackay, the first exhibition displayed 454 charts of information on families who were in Mackay before 1885. This display was held as part of the 2021 Heritage Festival, receiving great interest from the community, with 940 people attending.[1]

The charts were the culmination of several years research by MFHS volunteers. Most of the charts' subjects were of men's achievements although a small number described the endeavours of women. To further highlight the achievements of Mackay women, I took the opportunity to add women's stories from the most recent past, with the intention of promoting their achievements to a wider audience in the form of a book All women in this publication are deceased.

There have been many prominent women who have contributed to the Mackay community over many years. I want to highlight

---

[1] *Heritage Awards 2022: Award Winners* 2022, Mackay, Mackay Regional Council, viewed 1/07/2024 https://www.mackay.qld.gov.au/__data/assets/pdf_file/0009/296685/Heritage_Awards_Finalists_2022.pdf

at least some of these women. I have decided not to include the 'Woman from the Leap' story as I regard this story as a myth - the composite of a few different stories. The entry about Mary Ready briefly covers events that happened at The Leap, a district of Mackay.

I have been unable to find information about several women. Some of those women were Nurse Fyhn, a maternity nurse who managed a private hospital during the mid-1920s and 30s in Juliet Street, Mackay; Myrtle Caddy who was a shopkeeper in West Mackay; Matron Eva Dent, who was Matron at the Mackay Base Hospital; Ivy Hatfield and Matron Harvison of the Cromer Hospital; and a Presbyterian missionary; Elizabeth Donaldson, who served from 1890 to 1896 in the Mackay region. I may have inadvertently missed a woman of significance, unknown to me, who has not been included. I apologise for this and hope to include any women I have not included in a subsequent publication.

This book is a collective biography of thirty-seven women who made a significant contribution to the Mackay district from the 1860s to 2023. Their stories reflect the changing role of women in Australia from early settlement days to the present. These women who are now deceased, came from all walks of life. Whether it was their intention to make a mark on the Mackay and surrounding districts, they achieved acclaim for their efforts and together they portray a cross section of life as women who lived in the district from the 19th to 21st centuries.

The women were mostly from Great Britian or one of its colonies. Eight women were born in Mackay as well as another five women born in Queensland. Many of the women left behind family and the comforts of home, to make a perilous journey from overseas to Australia. They suffered isolation. They toiled to build a new life for their families in a tropical environment and many faced the challenges of colonial life along with the social and cultural changes and discrimination of those eras. Not all women had the same opportunity to contribute to society. Some women were less fortunate than others in their life experiences when either health issues, misfortune or even violence ended their lives. It has been difficult to find photographs of some women form the early days of settlement. Information about their lives was often not recorded, unless they came from wealthy or prominent families.

The history of women has not been recorded in the same way as that of men. In the past there has been less recognition of women's contribution to society and less written about women. To a certain extent, especially in past agricultural communities, women were largely 'invisible'. They were not the decision makers; they often went unnoticed in the community and were not written about in the media. Only the immediate family were aware of their contribution to the family and society. Women are now more 'visible', for example, women in business and sport are portrayed more often in the media, although equal pay for paid employment is yet to be achieved. The Australian Government is passing legislation to improve workplace gender equality.[2]

A biographical record of Queensland women was published in 1939 by Webb, Elliot and Company.[3] A Board selected Queensland women for a one-page entry describing their place of birth, level of education, philanthropic and charitable spheres and other interests. Some of the entries are quite brief. The women's backgrounds were from a wide range of endeavours, graziers, nurses and other distinguished careers. These women were mostly from European backgrounds. This publication reflects the life and times of the dominant European culture.

---

[2] Gallagher, Katy, 2024, 'Employer Gender Pay Gaps Published for the First Time', Department of the Prime Minister and Cabinet, viewed 6/12/2024 https://ministers.pmc.gov.au/gallagher/2024/employer-gender-pay-gaps-published-first-time

[3] *Biographical Record of Queensland Women : a Representation of Every Sphere Showing Activities and Interests, Social, Philanthropic, Historic, Scholastic, Sport and Travel* 1939, [Brisbane], The Company, viewed 13/08/2024 https://www.slq.qld.gov.au/blog/biographical-record-queensland-women-1939.

There have been several Australia-wide studies written about groups of women albeit, not many. One of those studies portrayed journalists who early in 1943, were selected by the Australian Government to undertake a promotional tour of eastern Australian military bases. 'The purpose of the tour was to gain publicity for the women's services with the aim of increasing enlistments to release servicemen to fight in New Guinea.'[4]

Another such study was that of a group of thirty-six female parliamentarians who were elected to the House of Representatives in the 1996 federal election. The number of women, (thirty-six); was an opportunity for Paul Pickering to examine the biographical characteristics of these women; - comparing their common experiences and backgrounds, as well as exploring the similarities and differences with previous members of the Coalition Members of Parliament. It was suggested that this group of women was a significant development in Australian politics.[5]

Several women's collective biographies published include a history of the South Australian Medical Women's Society,[6] stories about female pilots,[7] a book about great Australian women,[8] a bilingual collection of Italian Australian women's stories,[9] pioneering women of Australia's first fleet,[10] stories about some Australian Aboriginal

---

[4] Clarke, Patricia, 2020, 'In the Days of Print: Four Women Journalists in World War II', *Australian Journal of Biography and History*, v.12 no. 4, pp.3-28.

[5] Pickering, Paul, 1998-03, 'The Class of 96: A Biographical Analysis of new Government Members of the Australian House of Representatives', *The Australian Journal of Politics and History*, vol. 44 no.1, pp.95-112.

[6] South Australian Medical Women's Society, 1994, *The Hands of a Woman: South Australia's Medical Women's Society*, Kent Town, South Australia, Wakefield Press.

[7] Mexted, Kathy, 2021, *Australian Women Pilots: Amazing True Stories*, Sydney, New South Publishing.

[8] De Vries, Susanna, 2003, *The Complete Book of Great Australian Women: Thirty-six Women Who Changes the Course of Australia*, Pymble, N.S.W., Harper Collins.

[9] Kahan-Guidi, Anna Maria, Weiss, Elizabeth, 1990, *Give Me Strength: Forza e Coraggio: Italian Australian Women Speak: A Biographical Collection*, Broadway, N.S.W., Women's Redress Press.

[10] De Vries, Susanna, 1995, *Strength of Spirit: Pioneering Women of Achievement from First Fleet to Federation*, Alexandria, N.S.W., Millennium Books.

women,[11] biographies of ten significant women,[12] women traders in post war Hong Kong and Australia,[13] a tribute to Australian women and a book about Australia's funny women.[14]

A publication that reflects the changes that effected thirty-six women in Australian society from the colonial and federation eras to the present, who the author believes changed the course of Australia was written by Susanna De Vries.[15] Each woman has ten to twenty-five pages written about her in some detail. The tasks women undertook during those times were predominately labour intensive. For example, carrying water from the creek to the home, or working during the First and Second World Wars while the men were away. These women played a significant role in the way women were perceived and gave other women the confidence to become more independent.

A larger number of women (200), some well-known and others lesser known, born between 1762 and 1930 with none living by 1988, were selected for one-page biographies by editors for A Redress Anthology.[16] The authors were historians who researched women from many different backgrounds. These women had chosen a variety of careers from farming to business, politics, and science amongst many others.

Some were successful and some were not, but they demonstrated that women managed their own destiny and contributed to the Australian

---

[11] White, Isobel, et al., 1985, *Fighters and Singers: The Lives of Some Australian Aboriginal Women*, Oxford, Routledge.

[12] Fabian, Sue, 1983, *The Changemakers: Ten Significant Australian Women*, Milton, Qld., Jacaranda Press.

[13] Dickenson, Jackie, 2020-01, 'Splendid Opportunities: Women Traders in Postwar Hong Kong and Australia', *Australian Journal of Biography and History*, vol. 3, pp.63-78.

[14] Larkins, John and Howard, Bruce, 1976, *Sheilas: A Tribute to Australian Women*, Adelaide, Rigby.

[15] De Vries, Susanna, 2003, op. cit.

[16] Radi, Heather, 1988, 200 *Australian Women: Redress Anthology*, Broadway, NSW, Women's Redress Anthology.

history of women. Ten women who made a significant contribution to the lives of all Australians were selected in a group biography titled *The Changemakers: Ten Significant Australian Women*.[17] These women came from all walks of life from social reformers to conservatives. Unlike men, these women were not sculptured and placed in parks for everyone to notice and admire. These women included Elizabeth Macarthur, Caroline Chisholm, Catherine Helen Spence, Mary McKillop, Mary Gilmore, Vida Goldstein, Muriel Heagney, Elizabeth Kenny, Kath Walker, and Germaine Greer.

A collective biography of contemporary Australian women from all states of Australia was the focus of a tribute to women by John Larkins and Bruce Howard.[18] Some of these women were successful and famous while others were not. Some were unhappy and disadvantaged. It was a collection of biographies in the words of the women themselves. They enjoyed a variety of activities and occupations. The authors recorded that woman of colour mentioned the difficulties they encountered because of the colour of their skin.

A collection of stories about eventful lives and strong characters of Aboriginal women from fifteen communities in several states of Australia was written by anthropologists and others. The fifteen communities came from Cape York Peninsula, Arnhem Land and East Kimberley to the Western Desert, The Centre, South Australia, New South Wales and Victoria. Most of the essays were biographies although one was an autobiography. Each chapter contained from one to three biographies. This book offers a more intimate and personal view of these women and their lives.[19]

The Northern Territory Women's Register,[20] revised and expanded in 1991, contains only a few Aboriginal women for several

---

[17] Fabian, Suzane and Loh, Morag, op. cit.
[18] Larkins, John and Howard, Bruce, op. cit.
[19] White, Isobel et al, op. cit.
[20] Northern Territory Women's Advisory Council, 1991, *Northern Territory Women's Register 1948-1988*, Darwin, The Council.

reasons. Some of the barriers were distance, language, a lack of time, objections to the term bicentennial and the concept of the register. The women were nominated by members of the general community. They came from diverse ethnic backgrounds, career choices, and achievements. All women suggested to be in the register were accepted.

Two online databases hold biographical entries for women, those of the *Australian Dictionary of Biography* (ADB)[21] and the *Australian Womens Register* (AWR)[22]. The ADB has an article about colonial women.

The author, Barabra Dawson[23] includes stories about Indigenous women and those women who wrote about Indigenous women. The number of entries held by the ADB are approximately 13,00 with around 1,000 to 2,000 brief biographies of women. These entries are about women from all walks of life. The ADB is a national co-operative enterprise. It has a general editor based at the Australian National University, who liaises with working groups to select lists of names for inclusion. There are around 4,500 authors. Not all are academics. The ADB has several projects that will showcase specials projects.

The AWR was established in 1999 in collaboration between the University of Melbourne and the National Foundation of Australian women. 'It was created to build knowledge and recognition of the social, cultural, historical and economic contribution made by Australian women to public and private life.'[24] The AWR also showcases special groups of women in sports and other endeavours. The intention of the AWR is not to replace the ADB.

---

[21] Australian National University, 2024, *Australian Dictionary of Biography*, viewed 16/09/2024 https://adb.anu.edu.au/

[22] *Australian Women's Register*, 2024, viewed 16/09/2024 https://www.womenaustralia.info/entries/

[23] Dawson, Barbara, 2012, Colonial Women in the *Australian Dictionary of Biography*, viewed 16/09/2024 https://adb.anu.edu.au/essay/4

[24] *Australian Women's Register*, 2024, op. cit.

It is dependent on grants and donations, therefore, many worthy women who would have been included in the database are not.

The Group

One name that often occurs in the collective biographies of Australian women, is that of Dame Nellie Melba, soprano, who met and married her husband in the Mackay district. They had one son who was born there. I have written a brief biography about her experiences in the Mackay district at Marian. Melba had to argue with her father to be allowed to sing at concerts and charitable events although he did support her wish to have singing lessons in Paris. Her business skills allowed her to earn more money from the stock market than from her singing. She was her own manager and agent and was married and divorced. Her business and singing skills enabled her to become one of the world's first women to market her own talents to the greatest effect.[25]

Many women's achievements were either ignored or claimed by their husbands in colonial or early settlement days. The first cane harvester to be patented and operational in Brisbane, Queensland was designed in 1893 by Ada Fletcher.[26] Her husband, Joseph Fletcher was given credit for the 'cutting machine' in Easterby's book *The Queensland Sugar Industry*.[27]

There are also brief biographies of two musicians, Norma Shuttlewood, recipient of the Order of Australia, (OAM) and Pansy Wood. Each woman had a different introduction to the world of music. Shuttlewood learned singing, violin and piano as a child in Home Hill, Queensland, before moving to Mackay where she continued a lifelong interest in music, teaching and supporting other students in their musical careers. Wood's introduction to

---

[25] De Vries, Susana, 2003, op. cit. p. x.
[26] Kerr, Bill and Ken Blyth, 1993, *They're all half Crazy: 100 Years of Mechanical Cane Harvesting,* Brisbane, Canegrowers. p.14.
[27] Easterby, Harry T, 1932, *The Queensland Sugar Industry: An Historical Review,* Brisbane, Bureau of Sugar Experiment Stations, p.176.

music was more serendipitous, when the family won a piano in a raffle and her brother, the well-known Senator Ian Wood paid for her lessons. This inspired Wood in her passion for music, to teach and encourage others.

Marie Emma McBurney was an Australian artist who painted native plants of the Mackay region for over twenty-five years. She was the wife of the first Surgeon Superintendent of the Mackay Base Hospital. McBurney exhibited her art in England in 1884. Some of her artwork now hangs at Artspace, Mackay. Another artist, English born Annie Pring Marten lived briefly in the Mackay district before returning to England. Her outstanding artwork portraying early Mackay plantation life in 1876 depicted a lifestyle that has since vanished. The paintings were donated to the Mackay Regional Council by an English grandson.

An artist with the flair for becoming an entrepreneur was Cathy Knezevic, who displayed her skills by working firstly as an art assistant and then managing her own art gallery, Arthouse Gallery in Mackay. She was one of two women who successfully gained funding for an arts festival in the Whitsundays. Unfortunately, she did not live long enough to be involved in subsequent festivals.

For many women, who settled this country, when there were more men than women, marriage could be advantageous for both sexes. Jane Cooke (nee Harris) was one of many first-time female offenders transported to Van Dieman's Land in 1833 at the age of 21. She was convicted for minor theft, that of stealing a pair of stockings and cheese from her employer. Her accomplice did not sail with her. The initial sentence for stealing was seven years transportation to Van Dieman's Land. Harris married Francis Goude Cooke just two years after arriving, and her sentence was commuted. They had nine children. Francis Cooke was a publican in Launceston. Following his death Cooke moved to Mackay, Queensland. She applied for a publican's licence for the

Royal Hotel which was granted. Cooke proved to be a successful hostess, convening many social gatherings including more than one event for the Governor of Queensland.[28]

With dependent children, women in the early days needed a way of earning an income to support them. Some of these women took the opportunity to work in the hotel industry. Lebanese born, Mary Azar, was the Hotelkeeper for the Tattersalls Hotel (soon to be known as the Ambassador Hotel) in Mackay in 1936. Azar and her husband were successful haberdashers in Cairns before moving to Brisbane. On the death of her husband, Azar and some of her children moved to Mackay. Tattersalls Hotel, an old wooden building that had survived the 1918 cyclone, burnt to the ground. Azar sold off what she could and rebuilt the Art Deco style Ambassador Hotel, a landmark in Sydney Street today. The hotel was sold not long after it was built and brought Azar a healthy profit in 1938. It was resold again in 1951 for another substantial profit.

Barbra MacDonald sailed from Scotland in the 1860s, met and married her husband at Lake Elphinstone, 141 km south-west of Mackay. The couple managed a hotel in Mackay before applying for a hotelier's license in Walkerston, 11 km from Mackay. The couple had two sons who died in the first years of life. It was arduous manual labour for a single woman to run a hotel in colonial Queensland in the 1870s as well as dealing with patrons. McDonald extended the hotel to include a large hall where dances and concerts were held. The celebrated singer Nellie Mitchell or Dame Nellie Melba as she became known would sing in the hall. McDonald was owner and manager of the hotel for approximately thirty years until she died in 1901.

Amelia Cronin overcame significant disadvantage in her early life to become a successful hotelier. She was born in England and came to live in Australia in 1909. She lived and married in Maryborough

---

[28] Mackay Family History Society, 2012, 'Jane Cooke Hotelier 1865', Mackay, Queensland, The Society.

prior to applying for a hotel licence at the Grand Hotel, Sarina just south of Mackay. This was followed by an application for the Gargett Hotel just north of Mackay. During this time, she divorced her first husband Walter Charles Box which was unusual and difficult to achieve for the 1920s. It was expensive in that a private detective had to be employed, with torch light to observer the comings and goings of an errant husband visiting his mistress at night to 'catch them in the act'. The divorce was granted, even though the Judge said she was lucky to have it granted. Box then married Francis (Frank) Melody Cronin. The Family Court changed the divorce laws in 1975 to a 'no-fault' divorce.[29] With two families to support, another hotel was purchased in 1928 (the Railway Hotel, Marian) about 28 km north of Mackay, which proved a popular spot for visiting American servicemen. One further twist in the eventful life of Cronin was that only recently, thanks to DNA testing, her descendants learned that her foster-father was indeed her biological father.

Mary Ready, a native of Ireland, was the first European woman to live in Mackay, arriving by sailing ship in Sydney in 1855. Her husband with whom she had four children was also an Irishman she met in Sydney three years after she arrived. The Readys later became publicans after travelling by bullock wagon to Fassifern Station in Queensland. It was here that she gave birth under a bullock wagon to her second child, Kate. It was thought that she was the first European child born in the Mackay district. Ready also became entangled in the myth of the 'Woman of the Leap. Her husband James Ready, reportedly reared an Aboriginal girl that he rescued during an 'incident' at 'The Leap' where an Aboriginal person or persons were chased over a cliff (Mount Mandurana or previously known as Mt Johansburg) with a child in arms. It is not clear what happened, if this was a male or female who leaped from the cliff face or if this event happened at all or what the truth

---

[29] Edraki, Farz and Phillips, Keri, 2020, 'How Australia Introduced 'no-fault divorce': and why our Legal System is Under Review Again'. *ABC News*, viewed 3-10-2024 https://www.abc.net.au

was behind the rearing of this child, but the child was baptised Johanna Hazeldine (Judy).[30]

There were many Indigenous people in the Makay district at the time of settlement. These numbers quickly dwindled over time with the advance of European settlement. Reserves were established around 1877 until the numbers in the Reserves lessened and those people who identified as Aboriginal were transported to Palm Island while those who signed a paper to say they were non-Indigenous were allowed to stay in the district. Alternatively, they married a Pacific Islander and 'hid' their Aboriginal heritage. With the introduction of the sugar industry came the Pacific Islanders as labourers on sugarcane farms. Many Islanders married Aboriginal people `enabling them to remain in Australia rather than be repatriated to their homeland. This benefited those Pacific Islanders who preferred to stay in Australia following the introduction of the *Immigration Restriction Act* of 1901. This Act meant that many indentured Pacific Islanders were repatriated to their homeland unless they had an Australian family, had spent a lengthy period in Australia or other mitigating circumstance that allowed them to remain in Australia.

Rowena Trieve OAM was a descendant of an Australian Aborigine and a Pacific Islander. She was a granddaughter of Katie Marlla who was kidnapped by blackbirders and brought to Australia from Vanuatu in 1875. She was also cousin to Gloria Arrow who once worked for the Cook family at Greenmount Historic Homestead. Trieve was a businesswoman and representative of the Australian South Sea Islander community, who promoted their interests across the Mackay region. In recognition of her efforts, Trieve was awarded the Order of Australia in 2023. Gloria Arrow was a great-granddaughter of Katie Marlla. She suffered ill health as a child and spent most

---

[30] Moore, Clive, 1990, 'Blackgin's Leap: A Window into Aboriginal European Relations in the Pioneer Valley, Queensland in the 1860s' *Aboriginal History*, v.14, no.1, pp. 67-68.

of her working life as a housekeeper and caretaker for the Cook family at Greenmount. With the passing of the Cooks in the 1980s, Arrow became the focal point for tourists visiting the homestead. She was able to tell their dynastic story of settler life, and of her own cultural heritage.

Katie (Kitty) Marlla was a young 15-year-old when she and her female friend (Lucy Querro) were taken from a beach by the crew of a ship seeking workers for the Queensland cane fields. They were not given the choice of whether they wanted to be indentured workers. The girls were shackled until they reached Queensland where they initially worked in the cane fields. Life was physically arduous for Marlla. She was not entitled to the pension at age 67 so she leased five acres of land near Sunnyside, a district of Mackay, and with the aid of a mattock and hoe, grew sugar cane. Marlla became a devout Christian as did many of the Islanders when isolated from their family and local community. She believed that Australia was the land of opportunity for her and her growing family.[31]

Two women who made a significant contribution to the lives of Pacific Islanders and the Indigenous community were those of Mary Robinson and Elizabeth Martin both Anglican missionaries in the late 1800s. Robinson was born in India, of English military background. Her husband was a Major in the British Military Service at Fort William, West Bengal. He and his brothers had financial interests in Victoria, Australia which led him to be appointed as Manager of Branscombe Mill on the southside of the Pioneer River, Mackay. Mary Robinson was persuaded by Reverand Albert Alexander McLaren, from Holy Trinity Church in Mackay to offer a mission to educate Islanders and local Indigenous peoples in the English language, religion and culture. Robinson established the Selwyn Mission named after a former Anglican Bishop to the South Sea Islands at Te Kowai Plantation in 1882, at a site opposite Racecourse Mill. The mission changed

---

[31] Mackay Family History, 2012, 'Katy Marlla', Mackay, Queensland, The Society.

in location over the years between Marian and Te Kowai or Racecourse. Lessons in religious instruction were offered in Pijin English. Her work involved more than lessons; she became a carer to those who were unwell. Her home was always open to her students. 'She taught reading, writing and arithmetic and prepared men for baptism and confirmation'.[32] Men up to seventy and eighty in number walked 20 km every night for lessons often without a meal. Praise for her work came not only from her students but from farmers and clergy.

Elizabeth Martin was born in Scotland, arriving in Australia in 1846 with her husband whom she met in Scotland when he was on holiday from Mandurana, near Mackay. Martin donated a section of their land at Mandurana for an Anglican Mission and for an Anglican Church in 1882. Reverand McLaren was again the inspiration for Martin's work with the Islanders. St Peter's Church at Mandurana was built in 1884 with donations raised from the local community and a concert at the School of Arts, Wood Street, Mackay where Helen (Nellie) Mitchell performed. Melba provided further financial assistance when the church was damaged by cyclones. It is unclear for what period the Mission continued. St. Peter's Church is now heritage listed as is the cemetery where Robinson's husband and some of the Islanders were buried.[33]

Nolear Ramsamy, an Indigenous Australian was born at Port Liu on Prince of Wales Island in the Torres Strait. She had a large family, including three children prior to her marriage with 'Ramchandra', who was known locally as 'The Snake Man'. He collected vaccine from one of Australia's deadliest snakes, the taipan. As an Indigenous woman from the Torres Strait, she was a leader in her community. She had a menagerie of native

---

[32] Moore, Clive, 2017, *Making Mala: Malaita in Solomon Islands 1870s-1930s*, Canberra, ANU Press, p.153.

[33] Hall. Glenn, 2017, 'Mandarana: St Peters Churchyard Cemetery', Mackay History, viewed 20/11/2024 https://www.mackayhistory.org/research/cemeteries/mandarana_cemetery.html

animals at their property in Slade Point, Mackay, one of the beach suburbs. Ramsamy was well known locally and developed many friendships over her 100+ years.[34]

Several women in Mackay have contributed to their community by actively working to provide services and amenities. The advent of technology gradually freed women from many of the manual tasks that were time consuming. This was a gradual transition; it did not take place overnight. Before electricity was installed in the home, light was provided in the regions by cotton wicks floating in a saucer of mutton fat. Candle grease caused stains, and the smell was horrific resulting in more housework. The Brisbane district was the first to install electricity in around the mid-1920s.[35]

Mackay had electricity in 1924. Townsville, north of Mackay had a substation built in 1953, and electricity went out to Winton in 1963. Prior to electricity, gas lights proceeded the introduction of electric lights by forty years. The Mackay Gas Company was established in 1884. Kerosene lanterns and carbide lights were available to those people who did not have access to gas.[36] The introduction of refrigerators, obviated the need to preserve fruit and saved women time. Water piped to the kitchen and bathroom was another labour-saving device. Previously, water was carried from the creek to the house. The first washing machines, flat irons, vacuum cleaners and other devices coming onto the market, while crude, freed women from many manual tasks. These labour-saving devices freed up women's time and provided the opportunity for women to spend more time outside the home and in the community. Women who married into wealthy families

---

[34] Taracassidy, 2017, 'Mackay Royalty Turns 100, Still Catching Yabbies', *The Courier Mail,* 6 October, viewed 20/11/2024, https://www.couriermail.com.au/news/queensland/mackay/mackay-royalty-turns-100-still-catching-yabbies-news-story/a4e490ca74f114f5fde900476c4c58ee

[35] Williams, Raye, 1983, *An Electric Beginning: A History of Electricity Supply in the Mackay Region 1924-1983*, Mackay. Mackay Electricity Board.

[36] ibid. p.9.

often had domestic assistance in the house, but most women did not. For large families, the eldest daughter usually assisted with child rearing.

Mary Ann Sam (nee Sampson) was one of the first women to become involved in community life. Another was Eliza Jane Tanner. Sampson sailed from England in 1884 seeking employment as a domestic servant, arriving at Rockhampton. She met James Jung Sam, a farmer who was twelve years her senior. Choosing a partner of Chinese heritage in colonial North Queensland was unusual for a Northern European woman although Chinese men were known to be hard workers and to provide a regular income whereas European men were known to be fond of alcohol and often violent. They settled in the Mackay district and had twelve children. Sam was known as the 'Grand Old Lady of Northside'. She was regarded as a hard worker for the community, raising funds for World War I events, and assisting with events on Anzac Day. She was also a hard worker for the Northside Church of England. As a mother she supported her children's sports events. In recognition of her work for the community, a social housing complex was built at North Mackay and named *Mary Ann Sam*.[37]

Eliza Jane Tanner (nee Harrison) was a former Gympie resident. She came to Mackay in 1904 with her husband George Gutteridge. They had ten children which was common in the early 1900s, although not all lived to adulthood. Women often had careers and numerous children. Gutteridge, who married Walter Tanner in the last few years of her life, was a community worker for several charitable organisations. She was one of the earliest members of the Country Women's Association, Mackay Branch and, a member of the Women's Auxiliary Committee of the District hospital holding the office of President on at least one occasion.

---

[37] Watkins, Lillian, 2021, 'Mackay Social Housing Opens Up on Palmer St in North Mackay', *The Courier Mail*, viewed 18/10/2023 https://www.couriermail.com.au

She was a member of several other committees, owned her own home, and a T Model Ford which she drove.[38]

Miss Mary Finlay was the first female alderman on the Mackay City Council in 1937. Finlay was born in Mackay and had a brother who was also an alderman on council. Miss Finlay, as the name implies, never married. She was a staunch Labor supporter and campaign manager to William (Bill) Forgan Smith, long term Premier of Queensland (1887-1953), who was also the Member of the Legislative Assembly for Mackay. She was a Labor supporter all her life, and worked as a clerk for the Australian Workers Union, Mackay.[39]

Mary Ellen Struthers was elected as an independent alderman on the Mackay City Council in 1967. Struthers was born in Toowoomba and moved with her husband, initially to Proserpine, where they established a furniture business, then moving to Mackay in the 1950s. Struthers was well known for her community work. She founded 'Meals on Wheels', for which she worked tirelessly to raise funds. She was the first woman to serve on the Mackay Regional Electricity Board, (1967-1973). She achieved many of her goals to improve community life for Mackay citizens.[40]

There have been many women in the medical field who have contributed to the health and well-being of the Mackay community. Some of these include Margaret Mitchell Insch, a midwife, born in Scotland and sailed to Australia with her husband and children in 1883. Fortunately for Insch, an uncle in Scotland was a doctor who passed many skills onto her which stood her in good stead in the new country. She birthed ninety-nine babies and cared

---

[38] Patterson, Nita, 2021, 'Eliza Jane Gutteridge Formerly Harrison', Mackay, The Author, p.1
[39] 'After 27 Years Miss Finlay Retiring from A.W.U. Office', 1951, *Daily Mercury*, Friday 20 April 1951, p.2.
[40] 'Former Mackay Alderman Dies', 1988, *Daily Mercury*, 6 December, p.7.

for many sick people in the Pioneer Valley having settled in the Mirani district.[41]

Matron Barlow was an English born career nurse who trained in the Brisbane Children's Hospital around 1900 and later became Matron of the Ormond Private Hospital in Mackay by 1908. The Ormond Hospital was designed by Dr Charles Williams and was modern for its time. The land was viewed as ideal for a medical complex and in 1927 became the Mackay Mater Misericordiae Hospital which was open to the public until 1987. Matron Barlow married Albert Christensen, eight years her junior in 1914 and never practised nursing again. Barlow offered medical aid to residents but did not practice professionally. The reasons for this have not been identified but her marriage or the 'marriage bar'[42] seems to be the most likely reason.

Under the 'marriage bar' legislation, women who were employed in the Australian Public Service were required to give up their jobs once they married.[43]

Mary Jane Derrer, recipient of the Military Medal (MM), was born in Mackay of Swiss born parents. She and her sister Rosine

---

[41] Laskey, Alan, 2017, 'Pioneering Granny Insch Forged a Long Life in the Valley', viewed 2023-04-20 https://www.ancestry.com.au

[42] The Marriage Bar: The temporary lifting of the 'marriage bar' changed the employment opportunities available to married women. The bar was implemented in 1876 and required most female employees to resign from their posts upon marriage, forbidding the employment of married women in many cases. The bar was reinstated at the end of the war.
- Women were divided about whether married women should continue working at the end of the war. Isobel M Pazzey of Woolwich reflected a widely held view when she demanded that married women should be sent 'home to clean their houses and look after the man they married and give a mother's care to their children. Give the single women and widows the work.'
- The marriage bar was not permanently lifted until after the Second World War, and some parts of the Civil Service retained the bar until 1973. 'Changes to Women's Employment During the First World War', 2010, *The Postal Museum*, viewed 1/10/2024 https://www.postalmuseum.org/blog/working-women-during-wwi/

[43] Sawer, Marian, 2016, 'The Long, Slow Demise of the 'Marriage Bar', *Inside Story*, 8 December, viewed 20/09/2023 https://insidestory.org.au/

enlisted as nurses during World War I. Derrer embarked for Egypt in 1915 and treated wounded soldiers at Gallipoli and in France. Derrer was the survivor of a bombing by enemy aircraft, along with other nurses. They rescued wounded soldiers trapped in burning hospital tents. For her bravery she was awarded a Military Medal (MM). Derrer was discharged from the services due to injury in 1917 but rejoined until her discharge in 1920. She married and lived to the age of 93 years although she suffered from arthritis in later years.[44]

Dr. Berry, recipient of the Officer of the British Empire (OBE), was the first and only female surgeon and superintendent of the Mackay Base Hospital and was a much-loved member of the Mackay community. Born and educated in New Zealand, Dr Berry came to the Mackay Base Hospital in 1944. When Dr Berry had served her term at Mackay following World War II, there was a public outcry, and the Queensland Department of health reversed its decision to transfer her and appointed Dr Berry as Medical Superintendent in 1946. She was awarded the Officer of the Order of the British Empire (OBE) in 1964 for meritorious services to the citizens of Mackay. She held a top executive position in a man's world. She led by example with her high standard of professionalism and care. On her retirement to New Zealand in 1972, she was commended for her long-standing contribution to the Mackay community, of ex-servicemen and women and the Aboriginal and Islander communities.[45]

Still on the issue of health, a short life was marked by people's lack of knowledge about transmittable diseases. Hilda Finger was the fifth of ten children born to German-born parents. Born in an era when medical knowledge was limited (1891), Hilda was

---

[44] Mary Jane (Derrer) Gallager MM (1892-1986), 2023, *Wikitree*, viewed 20/5/2024 https://www.wikitree.com/wiki/Derrer-69

[45] 'Dr Annie Berry 1913-1998', 2012, *Mackay 150 1862-2012: Our people, Our Places, Our Stories*, Mackay, Mackay Regional Council. Viewed 20/05/2023 https://www.mackay.qld.gov.au/__data/assets/pdf_file/0010/125992/10_Unsung_Heroes_web.pdf

diagnosed with Leprosy at the age of nineteen, and was transported in a wooden crate from Mackay to Peel Island, a leprosy colony near Brisbane. By the age of twenty-five, Finger had a heart attack and died on the Island. The impact on her young life, and on that of her family, was due largely to ignorance about the disease and a lack of knowledge about how to treat the disease. Today, the disease can be treated, and the patient survive without shame and ostracism brought to a family.[46]

There were several female farmers in the district as distinct from graziers. Although the census data has not categorized groups of women as farmers, there have been several women farming in the Mackay district. A farmer has been described as a person who operates a farm and/or cultivates the land. An alternative definition is that of a person engaged in agriculture and the raising of living organisms for food or raw material. That is a broad scope as compared to another group of women who could be categorised as graziers. These people are described as rearing or fattening of sheep or cattle.[47]

There are four women whose role in life could be broadly described as that of a farmer. One such person was Margaret Coalter who was born in Scotland and arrived in Mackay with her family at the age of eight. Her father, William Coalter, took up a selection at what is now called Koumala and pursued a career with the Colonial Sugar Refining Company (CSR) in 1883. Coalter and an aunt managed the selection while her father worked at the sugar mill. Her skills were in dressmaking (self-taught), horsemanship, growing fruit, and vegetables and caring for livestock. She met and married Samuel Arbuthnot, a good-looking Irishman and they managed a property at Homebush another sugar growing district near Mackay. During her lifetime, Arbuthnot saw many changes

---

[46] Ludlow, Peter, 1996, *Peel Island*, p.159.
[47] Shepherd, Briana, 2019, 'The Female Farmers Taking a Stand to Change the Face of Australian Agriculture', *ABC News*, viewed 20/04/2023 https://www.abc.net.au/news/2019-08-24/visible-farmer-project-hightlights-the-rise-of-female-farmers/11442376

to the lifestyle and community from a landscape populated by Aboriginal peoples to the developed township of Mackay.[48]

Naomi Fudge and her husband Albert, sailed from London to Australia in 1884. Born in Somerset, England, the Fudges first tried tin mining with which Albert was familiar. Their first son was born on the tin mines at Kangaroo Hills south of Townsville, reported to be the first white baby boy born in the district much to the consternation of the Indigenous community. Naomi Fudge bought land and some cattle from the neighbours at Mirani to establish a dairy. Fudge became secretary of the local branch of the Australian Workers Union and began a catering business. She fostered a neighbour's baby son (Harry Penny) on the death of his mother in childbirth. It was not uncommon for a woman to die in childbirth and for families to foster a child in need. The fostered son and both families remain close to this day. The descendants of Penny still call the Fudges, aunt and uncle.[49]

Emily and Arthur Kemmis were amongst the earliest settlers in Mackay, taking up pastoral land at Oakendon, a sugar district of Mackay. Jamaican born and educated, Kemmis utilised her skills to open a private boarding house at her home in 1872-1880s. A tutor taught the children Latin, Greek and the classics, mathematics, French, geography, music and other subjects. The girls were taught needlework, and her classes were advertised in the local paper. The local government school was not opened until 1910.[50]

Maria Koch was born Maria Verena Meyer in Switzerland in 1844. At the age of 26, she sailed to Keppel Bay, near Rockhampton, at a time when many people were escaping the Franco-Prussian

---

[48] Koumala Presbyterian Women's Guild, [1974], *Historical Review of Koumala and District 1859-1974,* Mackay, Queensland, The Guild.
[49] Gcasandra, 2018, '10 Pioneering Women Who Shaped Mackay's Future', *The Courier Mail*, viewed 14/04/2023 http://www.couriermail.com.au
[50] Mackay Family History Society, 2012, 'Emily Slater Kemmis', Mackay, The Society.

War. She met and married Joseph Koch, a blacksmith of Mackay. The couple had six children and for thirty-eight years, Koch managed the farm after her husband died. She was an excellent horsewoman a regular church goer and friend to the Australian Pacific Islander community.[51]

Women who married into the Atherton and Cook families made a lasting contribution to the local community. The Atherton, Ross and Cook families were first based in New South Wales until they purchased grazing and investment properties around the Mackay and Cairns districts in Queensland. Letitia Orr was born in Ireland and sailed to Brisbane with her brother, Richard in 1868. Her soon to be brother-in-law, John Atherton, was an early explorer and settler of the Cairns district after whom the Atherton Tableland was named. Atherton and her husband had extensive holdings in the Mackay district and owned land that became the Plane Creek Milling Company. They were also philanthropists to their local community. Atherton taught her eight children at home up to the secondary level after which they received individual instruction from a private school tutor. Vida Althea, a daughter of Letitia and Richard Atherton, became the wife of Albert Cook, thus amalgamating the two grazing dynasties. It is believed that Vida met her future husband and his sister Ethel at school. Children from the grazier families, were initially home schooled before attending private schools in Mackay and New South Wales unlike many other families whose children attended local schools.[52]

Elizabeth Ross from Ross-shire in Scotland, sailed to Australia in 1856. Both the Ross and Cook families were graziers in the Armidale district of New South Wales. Ross married John Cook in 1860. Her brother Louis Ross had an agreement with John Cook

---

[51] *Daily Mercury*, 1937, 'The Passing of a Pioneer', Friday 26, p.9. viewed 9/02/2024, http://nla.gov.au/nla.news-article170261896
[52] Bowden, Vicky, 2021, 'Home education is an Old Concept with New Challenges', *Daily Mercury*, 17 February, viewed 7/05/2024 http://www.dailymercury.com.au

that they share ownership of land that they both had purchased. Therefore, John Cook became the owner of Balnagowan near Mackay when Louis Ross accidently drowned crossing a river on horseback. Cook often managed the New South Wales property in her husband's absence as well as managed their children, a life not uncommon for early settler women. Washing clothes near the riverbank had a disastrous outcome for Cook when her four-year-old daughter's dress caught alight from an open fire, and the child was burnt. Medical assistance was not immediate, and the child died from her injuries. These were not uncommon occurrences for those times.[53]

Vida Althea Atherton married Albert Cook, one of Elizabeth and Tom Cook's sons, in 1908, taking a three-month honeymoon to New South Wales where they travelled extensively. Cook dabbled in water colour paintings and trained briefly as a nurse before she returned to Mackay to marry. What was unique about Vida Atherton was that she kept a diary that described her life and times when she was growing up in Mackay. She followed her father in this trait, as Richard Atherton also kept a diary. The joining of these two successful families (Cook and Atherton) added to the Cook dynasty which culminated in the marriage of Cook's son Tom with Dorthy Drysdale. This union did not produce children, so Dorothy generously made a significant philanthropic donation of cash and property to the people of Mackay, Queensland and to international charities.[54]

Ethel Glenny, sister to Albert Cook, was a socialite, artist and traveller in keeping with the lifestyle of this wealthy family. As a young woman in an era when opportunities for a career were not as accessible as today, Glenny enjoyed the lifestyle of

---

[53] Clark, Betty, 1992, *A House Well Filled*, Mackay, Mackay Printing & Publishing, pp. 22-23.
[54] Bowden, Vicky, 2020, 'Mackay History: The Last Lady of Greenmount Homestead', *The Courier Mail*, October 1, viewed 15/03/2024 https://www.couriermail.com.au/news/queensland/mackay/mackay-history-

a wealthy young widow living on Sydney's north shore for most of her life.[55]

Beryl Neilsen OAM was also a widow and grazier who, when her husband died at the age of 46 years, sold her stake in their Winchester Downs property and established the John & Beryl Neilsen Winchester Downs Foundation in 2011. Not having any children of her own, Neilson took a great interest in the education of children, especially those from regional areas of Queensland.[56]

Unlike many of the women in this group, Marily Wallman was not afforded the opportunity of a long life. She was abducted and murdered by person or persons unknown in 1972 aged 14, when riding her bicycle along a quiet country road to the bus stop before travelling to high school. A small fragment of her skull was found in 1974. The impact on the small local community was enormous as was the loss and devastation felt by the family. No one has been charged with her murder, so the case is still open, and the family do not have closure. The response by the community after assisting in the initial search, was to drive or walk their children to school, not allowing them to go out unsupervised. It put fear into a community that had not known it before and has since changed the way in which many Australians transport their children to school.[57]

The role of women has changed greatly since the late 1800s. Women won the right to vote, and women have become better educated especially since 1975 when education was made free at the undergraduate level. Women are now choosing when they want to have children and/or a work life. Granddaughters are now

---

[55] Clark, Betty, 1992, op. cit. p. 24.
[56] Whiting, Melanie, 2021, 'Moranbah Grazier and Philanthropist Beryl Neilsen Awarded the OAM', *Daily Mercury*, June 13, viewed 20/04/2024 https://www.couriermail.com.au/news/queensland/mackay/moranbah-grazier-and-philanthropist-beryl-neilsen-awarded-oam/news-story/e743770561f29b788796ba195e35f44d
[57] Hegarty, Laura and Meecham Philpot, 2014, 'How Marilyn Wallman's Disappearance Changed Mackay', *ABC Local*, 11 February, viewed 13/01/2021 https://www.abc.net.au

entering university and aspiring to do exciting work that was not offered to their grandmothers. Women are becoming more the decision maker now than they ever have been.

The achievements of this group of women have laid the foundations for future generations to prosper. Many of these women lived through wars and depressions and have watched on as a little port town changed into the sugar capital of Australia and now a vibrant coal exporting, and sugarcane producing city.

Background

Mackay

Lieutenant James Cook, an English explorer landed on the east coast of Australia in 1770 aboard the *HMS Endeavour*. Europeans settled Australia for the purpose of establishing a penal colony. Queensland was initially a British administered Colony of New South Wales. It was settled by Europeans in 1825 as a location for the most difficult convicts. The closing of the penal settlement in 1839 was the opportunity for permanent settlement. Queensland separated from the Colony of New South Wales in 1859 and became the Colony of Queensland. On January 1, 1901, the Commonwealth of Australia was proclaimed. The Aboriginal people have been living in Queensland, Australia for many thousands of years prior to European settlement.[58]

With exploration of Queensland, the mouth of the Pioneer River and the Pioneer Valley was mapped by John Mackay in 1860.[59] During his travels, Mackay crossed the Pioneer River near Blacks Creek — part of which is now included in the Parish of Mia Mia.[60] As historian Clive Moore notes, …'the view from the top of Eungella Range was one of rich alluvial soil that swept down the Pioneer Valley to the sea. To the southeast was Connor's Range and northwards, Clarke's Range. To the east were the beginnings of Cattle, Black Waterhole, Blacks and Stockyard Creeks, which meet to form the Pioneer River.'[61]

---

[58] AIATSIS, 2024, 'First Peoples of Australia', viewed 23/05/2024 https://aiatsis.gov.au/explore/first-peoples-australia

[59] Mackay, John, 1860, 'Journal of John Mackay', *The Armidale Express*, 22-29 September, pp.2-3.

[60] Nardella, Kaye, Senior Curator, Museum of Lands, Mapping and Surveying, Department of Natural Resources and Mines, Queensland Government confirmed this by email on 28 October 2014.

[61] Moore, Clive, 1985, Moore, Clive, 1985, *Kanaka: A History of Melanesian Mackay*, Port Moresby, University of Papua New Guinea Press, p.101.

In the 1860s the Aboriginal people were still living in the Pioneer Valley and on the surrounding islands. By 1877, these people were forced to settle in a large reserve. Up until then, the Pioneer Valley, coastal mangroves, fertile plains and the rainforest had provided their food and shelter. Many of the local Indigenous people, the Yuibera, were displaced from Mackay to Palm Island in 1922.[62]

From 1863 onwards, Pacific Islanders had been recruited or black birded as labourers to work in the Queensland sugarcane fields or as domestic workers. The *Pacific Islanders Labourers Act* of 1901, meant that the Pacific Islanders were returned to their homeland, sometimes separating them from their families in Australia.[63] By 1908, the Pacific Islanders were repatriated unless they had been granted permission to remain in Australia. The descendants of the Pacific Islanders, (Australian South Sea Islanders) are recognised as a distinct cultural group within Australia.[64] Many have shared Indigenous and Pacific Islander heritage.

Although Pacific Islanders, Torres Strait Islanders, Aboriginal people, and other nationalities; the Italian, Maltese and others worked in the sugarcane industry around Mackay, the greatest number of immigrants came from the United Kingdom.[65] This is in part due to the White Australia Policy, an outcome of the *Immigration Restriction Act* implemented in 1901 by the first federal government which limited non-British migration. The Whitlam Government eliminated it in the 1970s with the introduction of legislation and policies such as the *Racial Discrimination Act* of 1975.[66]

---

[62] Ah-Wong, Wayne, 2007, 'Living Between Cultures: Reflections of Three Mackay Elders: Aboriginal, Torres Strait Island and South Sea Island Residents of Mackay from the 1930s to 2000', PhD thesis, Central Queensland University, p.24.
[63] National Archives of Australia, 2024,' South Sea Islanders', viewed 14/12/2024, https://www.naa.gov.au/help-your-research/fact-sheets/south-sea-islanders
[64] ibid.
[65] Australian Bureau of Statistics, 1981, *Census of Population and Housing: Characteristics of Persons and Dwellings in Local Authority Areas, Statistical Divisions, and Statistical Reports, Birthplace,* 1981, viewed 15/08/2016,
[66] White Australia Policy, 2024, *National Museum of Australia,* viewed 8/10/2024 https://www.nma.gov.au/defining-moments/resources/white-australia-policy

By late 1861, pastoral holdings dominated the landscape except for areas set aside from the Cape Palmerston and Balnagowan runs to make available urban land for Mackay and surrounding agricultural lands. Crops grown at that time were maize, tropical fruits and some sugarcane.[67] Pastoralism was supplanted by agriculture throughout the Pioneer Valley within twenty years of settlement. Pastoralism was only found around the foothills by 1883. Cattle proved to be more productive than sheep in this environment.[68]

Mackay today is a tropical sugarcane growing district with a population of around 127,000. The district no longer relies on the sugar industry as its main source of income but rather the coal mining industry to the north, west and south.

---

[67] Ah-Wong, Wayne, op. cit., p.24.
[68] Mackay Regional Council, 2024,' History of the Mackay Region', viewed 13/04/2024 https://www.mackay.qld.gov.au/about_council/your_council/history/history_of_the_mackay_region

Map of Central Queensland

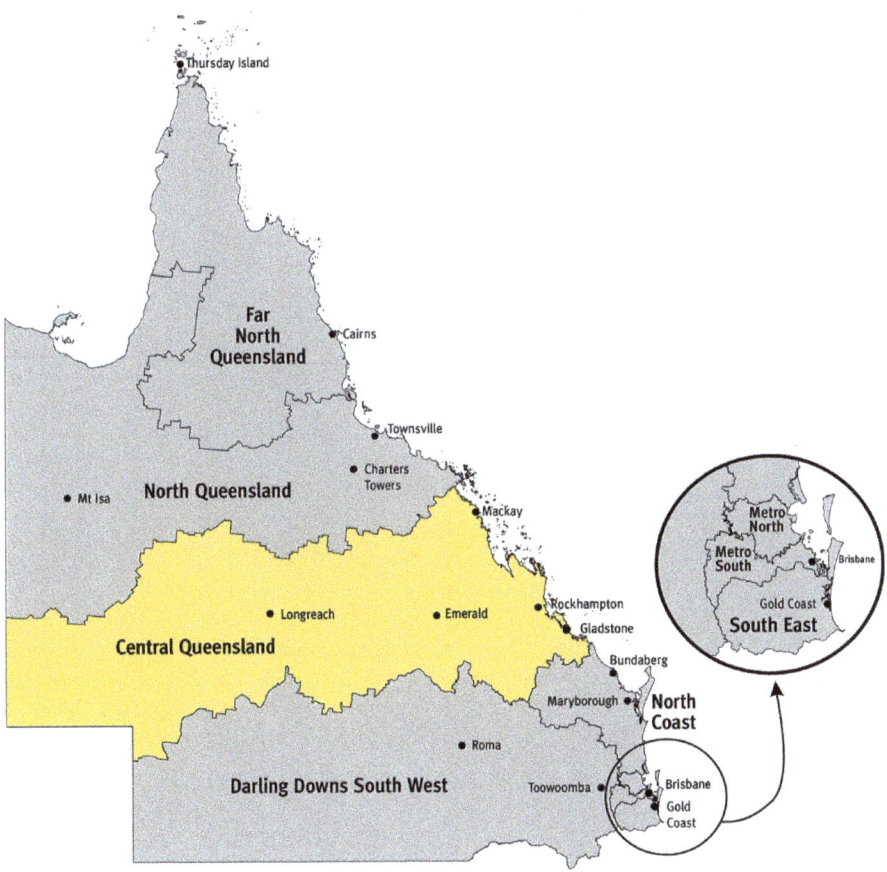

Figure 1 Central Queensland, Australia. Map courtesy of the Department of Education, Teach Queensland, Queensland Government.

Biographies
Arbuthnot, Margaret (1874–1959)

Figure 2 Margaret Coalter. Courtesy of Helen Onopko.

Born:
- 1 June 1874
- Linwood, Renfrewshire (Linwood), Strathclyde, Scotland, United Kingdom.

Died:
- 29 October 1959
- Mackay, Queensland

Occupation:
- Early settler and farmer of the Koumala and Homebush districts.

Alternative Name/s:
- Margret Coalter

Summary:

Margaret Coalter was an assisted passenger at the age of 8 when she arrived in Mackay with her family. It was a difficult and adventurous sixteen-week voyage, aboard the vessel *Scottish Knight*, leaving Glasgow on 15th July and arriving in Mackay on 2 November the same year.[69] Her parents William (born in Fermanagh, Northern Ireland) and Sarah Hunter Coalter were married in Kilbarchan, Renfrew, Scotland in 1874. Her sister Mary Jane was six years old on arrival in Mackay. Her father had married for a second time after the death of his wife, to Maria Spiers (Spears), prior to embarking for Australia.[70] Her half-sisters Agnes (3), and Rebecca (an infant) accompanied them on the voyage to Mackay. Unfortunately, Rebecca died in 1884.[71] A step aunt, Agnes Gallagher Spiers (Spears), accompanied them on their voyage.

The heat of tropical north Queensland was not suitable for the tight clothes they were wearing, and the absence of cooling devices was in stark contrast to Scotland from where they had come. They did not have accommodation or employment at the time of their arrival. The two Scottish women were unsuited for the type of life in which they found themselves.[72]

William Coalter soon found employment with the Colonial Sugar Refining Company (CSR) at the *Homebush Sugar Mill*

---

[69] Queensland Government, 1882, *Assisted Immigration 1848 to 1912-C*, viewed 15/11/2023 https://www.data.qld.goc.au/dataset/assisted-immigration1848-1912......

[70] *Deaths in the District of Mackay in the State of Queensland*, 1924, 'William Coalter', Mackay, Queensland, The Government.

[71] Ancestry, 1985, Australia, *Death Index*, viewed 20/11/2023 https://www.ancestry.com.au

[72] Living conditions in those days were primitive, cooking was done on an open fire, bread was baked in a camp oven and water for household had to be carried from a nearby creek. Kerosene lamps were a luxury, and, in many instances, people used 'fat lamps' which were made by filling a pannikin with tallow and inserting a wick made from a piece of stout cloth down the centre into the tallow. Comment from Sally Arbuthnot Chambers in a 1976 speech to the Mackay Business and Professional Women's Club, Mackay.

which began crushing in September of 1883.⁷³ He then took up a selection at Kelvin Grove (later Koumala) and on Margaret's 12th birthday, the family moved to their new home by bullock wagon with the assistance of an Indigenous man named Seekus.⁷⁴

Coalter continued to work at Homebush Sugar Mill and visited the family regularly, making the journey 40 miles each way on horseback to his selection.⁷⁵ It was a requirement that to own a selection, someone in the family had to live on the property. 'No habitation existed along the forty-mile route in those days except a hut on the bank of Plane Creek, known as Dick Paton's humpy.'⁷⁶ The creeks did not have bridges to cross and the road was only a dirt track. Aboriginals roamed the bush and called on the settlers with the request to 'Give-it flour, give it sugar?'⁷⁷

It was Margaret Coalter who showed her initiative by establishing a life for the family. She obtained meat from Kelvin Grove Station about a quarter of an hour's ride from their selection and met the coach that arrived from Mackay once a week. This was their main contact with civilisation. She planted vegetables, and fruit trees, managed fowls, and looked after the cattle and horses her father obtained. She became a good horsewoman with the experience she gained on the few saddle horses they owned, much to her pride and joy.⁷⁸

The Koumala Provisional School was proposed in 1888 and established in 1889 under the tuition of Mr Hatfield with 20 children registered.⁷⁹ Prior to that, The Government Surveyors wife, Mrs Burbank, who was a talented woman, had gathered

---

[73] Hall, Glen, 2929, 'Homebush Sugar Mill 1883-1922', viewed 23/11/2023 http://mackayhistory.org/research/sugar_mills/homebush.html
[74] Koumala Presbyterian Women's Guild, [1974], *Historical Review of Koumala and District 1859-1974*, Mackay, The Guild, p.35.
[75] Mackay Family History Society, 2012, 'Margaret Coalter 1882', The Society.
[76] Koumala Presbyterian Women's Guild, op. cit., p.36.
[77] ibid.
[78] ibid.
[79] ibid.

the local settler's children together and organised play acting and concerts, in which Coalter took an active part. 'The Burbank family had a governess – a highly educated and cultured English lady – who exerted a lasting influence on the young girl's life.'[80]

With the birth of Maria in 1885, it was decided to move the mother and younger children closer to the Homebush State School, which was established in 1889. This meant that Coalter at the age of 14, was left on the farm with her step-aunt. She took on the responsibility of the selection's upkeep. This involved making the family's clothes by hand, not having a sewing machine meant mostly working at night in the light of a 'fat lamp' (a wick in a tin filled with tallow which gave off a spluttering yellow light). Her inspiration for 'fashion' ideas was thought to have come from observations of attire worn by coach passengers.[81]

Coalter lived for seven years on her father's property at Koumala, approximately 50 km south of Mackay. Five of those years were spent with her step aunt in an isolated part of the tropical Queensland bush until she met a young good-looking Irishman, Samual Arbuthnot who decided that life would be without meaning unless he shared it with Margaret. Samuel was the son of Alexander Arbuthnot and Martha Shaw, born near Cookstown in County Tyrone, Northern Ireland in 1871. He had arrived in Mackay in 1886 and was employed to supervise Islander gangs working for the Colonial Sugar Refining Company (CSR) in the Homebush area.[82]

Coalter rejoined her family at Homebush when she was 19 and at 21, she married Samuel Arbuthnot on the 16 October 1895.[83] Samuel Arbuthnot was the son of Alexander and Mary Anderson Arbuthnot born in Brigh Townland, County Tyrone, Ireland

---

[80] Mackay Family History Society, 2012, 'Margaret Coalter 1882', op. cit., p1.
[81] ibid.
[82] 'Mr Samuel Arbuthnot', 1947, *Daily Mercury*, viewed 3/04/2024 http://nla.gov.au/nla.news-article171091961
[83] Mackay Family History Society, 2012, op. cit.

on 26 October 1859. The Arbuthnot's had four children; Sarah Hunter Arbuthnot Chambers (3 August 1896); John Alexander Arbuthnot (15 September 1897); Isabella Mary Arbuthnot Jones (21 December 1906); and Margaret Coalter Arbuthnot Epplere (20 January 1914).[84] Initially the family lived in a tent until they took up a selection at Ardtrea Farm, Homebush, farming for almost forty-eight years in the production of raw sugar.

Both the Arbuthnotts were associated with the building of the first Presbyterian Church at Homebush, which was subsequently demolished by the 1918 cyclone. At the couple's sixtieth wedding anniversary in 1945, Arbuthnot recalled many memories of the early days in Homebush. She saw the first CSR tram lines laid from Bakers Creek to Homebush. She also remembered the machinery for the mill being brought to the terminus at Bakers Creek by teams and conveyed by horse trollies to Homebush over the newly laid tramline. She watched the building of Homebush Sugar Mill in 1883 and saw it demolished eight years later. The bricks were later used for other local buildings.[85] Their only son, John Alexander, managed the property when they retired to Mackay.[86] Margaret Arbuthnot died in the Lister Hospital Mackay on 29 October 1959, the seventy-seventh anniversary of her arrival in Australia and was buried in the Mackay City Cemetery.

Events:

- 1882 Arrived in Mackay

---

[84] *Deaths in the District of Mackay in the State of Queensland,* 1959, 'Margaret Arbuthnot', Queensland Government.
[85] Mackay Family History Society, 2012, 'Margaret Coalter 1882', op. cit.
[86] 'Golden Wedding: Mr and Mrs Arbuthnot', 1945, *Daily Mercury*, Monday 15 October, p.2., viewed 22/11/2023 http://nla.gov.au/nla.news-article170630670

Arrow, Gloria Jean (1941-2021)

Figure 3 Gloria Arrow at Greenmount Homestead circa 1958. Photograph courtesy of *Facebook*.

Born:
- 17 February 1941
- Queensland, Australia

Died:
- 9 May 2021
- Mackay Queensland.

Occupation:
- Houskeeper and caretaker at Greenmount Homestead, Walkerston, Mackay, Queensland. In later years, Arrow became a guide to tourists and a tourist attraction in her own right whilst living at Greenmount Historical Homestead.

Alternative Name/s:
- Gloria Arrow

Summary:

Gloria Arrow was the great-granddaughter of Katie Marlla who was kidnapped from Ambae Island, Vanuatu and brought to Mackay in 1875 to work in the sugarcane fields. Her parents were Alan and Kathleen Arrow from Homebush near Mackay. One of ten children, she suffered with ill health as a child, firstly with bronchitis and then poliomyelitis. One effect of the disease was that she spent at least six months in hospital under the care of Dr Berry and missed schoolwork which she could not catch-up. By the age of 13, school was behind her.

Arrow worked briefly for a few months in outback Australia at Darr River Downs Homestead near Longreach, after which she returned to Mackay and gained employment at Greenmount Homestead as a housemaid. Arrow began working for the Cooks in 1958 at the age of 17. She was a live-in maid, and later the housekeeper and caretaker for them both until 1983 when the property closed. In that year, Arrow celebrated sixty years living at Greenmount Homestead.[87]

Greenmount Homestead was owned and managed by Tom and Dorothy Cook who inherited the property from Albert Alfred and Vida Althea Cook. Alfred employed an architect and built the homestead in 1914-15 for his new wife. The Greenmount property formed part of the original claim for land by Captain John Mackay following his exploration of the Mackay district in 1860.[88]

Duties undertaken by Arrow at the Homestead were many and varied including housework, being a companion to Dorothy Cook

---

[87] Miko, Tara, 2021, 'Tributes Flow for Greenmount Homestead's former Caretaker Gloria Arrow', *The Courier Mail*, viewed 3/05/2024 https://www.couriermail.com.au/news/queensland/mackay/tributes-flow-for-greenmount-homesteads-former-caretaker-gloria-arrow/news-story/08fccc71f733347b4522bed7568c3b89

[88] Mackay Regional Council, 2016, 'Welcome to Greenmount Homestead: Self-Guided Tour', viewed 21/04/2024 https://www.mackay.qld.gov.au/__data/assets/pdf_file/0003/104844/Greenmount_Brochure.pdf

and Hannah Drysdale (Dorothy's mother) when they travelled to Mackay for shopping or the lady's hairdresser, and also as a model for the days Greenmount Homestead sponsored fashion parades as well as a general 'help'. There were rules established for Greenmount domestic staff drawn up by Vida Cook. Those rules were:

- Every day: Early tea at 6.30 am, sweep and dust the dining room, verandahs and office
- Breakfast at a quarter to 8 am followed by general housework until morning tea at 10:30am
- Dinner was at 12:30 pm
- Afternoon tea was at a quarter to 4pm
- Monday and Tuesday: Wash, iron and scrub kitchens
- Wednesday: living and two bedrooms a thorough clean
- Thursday: Dining rooms
- Friday: Clean silver and some windows
- Saturday: Offices, bathroom, pantry, and kitchen and soak down clothes
- Cobweb verandahs once a month[89]

With the passing of the Cooks in the 1980s, the property was gifted to the Mackay Regional Council along with more than 20,000 historical items. Arrow, with her knowledge of the house, and as a caretaker of sixty years, suggested looking in the attic for items when an exhibition was to be held. Historical items found in the attic included horse racing trophies, panoramic photographs from the 1860s, and a reproduction of Tom Roberts's work, *Shearing the rams*, which he had hand signed.[90] It was reported that Albert and Vida Cook had bought the print on their honeymoon in 1908. Arrow said items that were not required for immediate use were

---

[89] This notice was in the handwriting of Vida Cook and pinned to the front door of the room used by Gloria Arrow when she lived at Greenmount Homestead. Also included in the notice with the handwritten list was a transcript.

[90] Maddison, Melissa, 2018, 'Hidden Loft at Historic Greenmount Homestead Uncovered on Tip by Caretaker', *ABC Tropic North*, viewed 17/03/2023 https://www.abc.net.au/news/2018-05-27/long-forgotten-loft

stored in the loft. 'Anything we did not want to use, the household items, all just went in the loft. In summer, in the days when we didn't have electricity, we'd use iron fold-out beds to sleep on the verandahs, instead of in the rooms, to get the cool breeze at night. So, when they were not needed, the loft is where they went.'[91]

The homestead is now a museum with bedrooms, sitting and dining rooms set up as if the family were still living in the property. Arrow was the caretaker for more than sixty years until her retirement into Mackay. An exhibition was held, Conversations with Gloria on the Verandah, with artist Janet Ambrose and photographer Kealie Frerichs taking the time to explore the history of the homestead through her eyes. Arrow's comment about the Cooks was that: 'They had time for their staff, they were really like parents, and they looked after all the staff.'[92] Dorothy Cook regarded Arrow as a family member, taking her to see the Doctor when she had bronchitis.[93]

Inevitably, a valuable link to Mackay's pioneering past was severed with the passing of Gloria Arrow, as mentioned by George Christensen in Federal Parliament. Christensen, former member for Dawson, described her as so much more to the Cooks than the role of live-in housemaid that she undertook at 17 years of age. She became more of a daughter, carer of Tom and Dorothy as well as to Hannah, Dorothy's mother. Provision was made for Arrow to stay at the property for as long as she chose.[94] Arrow was remembered for her longstanding association with Greenmount Homestead and her kind-hearted manner which made her an esteemed member of the community. Jan Smith, a

---

[91] ibid.
[92] Charles, Caitlan, 2019, 'Time to Leave the Historic Home of More Than 60 Years', *Cairns Post*, viewed 17/03/2023 https://www.cairnspost.com.au/queensland/mackay
[93] ibid.
[94] Christensen, George, 2021, *Arrow, Ms Gloria Jean: Speech*, House of Representatives, Parliamentary debates, Monday 24 May, viewed 17/03/2023 https://openaustralia.org.au/debate/

former Mackay journalist, wrote a book about Arrow describing her as housekeeper, friend, confidant, and 'daughter' to Tom and Dorothy Cook.[95]

Arrow died on May 9, 2021, at the age of 80 years. She was buried in Walkerston Cemetery.

Events:

- 1958 Began work at Greenmount Homestead
- 2019 Retired from Greenmount Historical Homestead

Links:

Conversations with Gloria Arrow http://www.janetambrose.com/gal-Gloria.php

Figure 4 Gloria Arrow 2018
Photograph courtesy *ABC Tropical North*.

---

[95] Smith, Jan, 1998, *The Dark Daughter: A Mackay Story*, Mackay, Quick Printers.

Atherton, Letitia Jane (1849-1934)

Figure 5 Letitia Jane Atherton. Photograph courtesy of Greenmount Historic Homestead.

Born:
- 18 January 1849
- Strabane, County Tyrone, Northern Ireland.

Died:
- 4 April 1934
- Brisbane, Queensland.

Occupation:
- Early settler, grazier, and philanthropist. Atherton faced many of the dangers early female settler encountered when living in a tropical environment without the assistance of modern medical facilities.

Alternative Name/s:
- Letitia Jane Orr

Summary:

Letitia Jane Orr was the only daughter of Reverand John Samuel Corbett Orr and Mary Martin of Northern Ireland. She sailed to Australia aged 19 sharing a second-class cabin with her older brother Richard (21) aboard the *Winterthur,* leaving the Port of London on 26 August 1868 and arrived at Brisbane 20 December of that year.[96] Richard Orr matriculated in Arts at Queens College, Belfast Ireland, and gained tutoring experience in Ireland and Queensland before attaining the position of Headmaster at Tingalpa a suburb of Brisbane.

Letitia Orr married Richard Atherton, son of Edmund and Esther Atherton on the 23 July 1870.[97] Richard's parents sailed from Lancashire, England in 1844 and settled in the Armidale area of New South Wales. John Atherton, brother of Richard, was a bushman, explorer, farmer, and early settler of the Cairns district having the Atherton Tablelands named after him. Letitia and Richard had ten children between 1871 and 1888, eight (four boys and four girls) of whom survived to adulthood. Letitia and Richard raised their young children firstly at their property, Woonon near Sarina and then at Howard Park south of Mackay which encompassed the Mackay Airport and Bakers Creek areas.

Richard Atherton during his lifetime was one of the early pastoralists. He owned family property in conjunction with his father and brother-in-law. These properties included West Hill station in 1863 located midway between St Lawrence and Mackay. He stocked the property with cattle from Mount Hedlow. In 1865 due to the loss of cattle speared by the Indigenous people and disease, cattle were moved to Plane Creek Station near Mackay

---

[96] Shipping records indicate that Letitia was 21 and Richard 23 when they arrived in Australia, but Letitia would have been 19 and not 21 as cited on the shipping records for the *Winterthur*.

[97] Gcasandra, 2018, '10 Pioneering Women Who Shaped Mackay's Future', *The Courier Mail*, 3 March, pp. 12-13, viewed 17/03/23 https://www.couriermail.com.au/news/queensland...

(owned by Richard and his brother Edmund and E Bell) and West Hill was abandoned. Richard and Letitia established the property Woonon where some of the children were born. Vida Athaea was one of those.

The Atherton family had extensive holdings and gave security over their freehold lands to the Queensland Government. The government established the Plane Creek Central Sugar Mill Company (now owned by Wilmar Sugar). They held *Howard Park* where the younger children were born, Plevna Station on the Eungella Range, Sutton Creek Station, and Mount Funnell Station, about 50 miles south of Mackay. As well as having properties the family were generous to their community.

The Atherton's had eight children who lived to adulthood; Richardina Binny Orr Atherton (1871-1960); Letitia Emily Alice Atherton (1873-1962); Vida Althaea Atherton Cook (1875-1955; Reginald Oscar Atherton (1878-1969); Alan Rupert Atherton (1880-1966); Rosamund Brenda Atherton (1882-1974); Arnold Howard Atherton (1888-1964); and Aubrey Howard Atherton (1888-1964). Aubrey died in June and Arnold died in December of the same year.[98] The children were born at a time when Mackay was first settled so there may have been a mid-wife in attendance for the births.

The children's education was undertaken firstly by their mother then at the secondary level, they were sent to the George Perkins Private School in Mackay. George Perkins had matriculated from Oxford University and arrived in Australia in 1883. The George Perkins Private School specialised in individual instruction for various business examinations and guided them for entrance to private schools in the south. The Atherton children attended this school at the same time as Albert and Ethel Cook. A fortuitous meeting for both Albert and Vida who would later marry.[99]

---

[98] *Deaths in the District of Brisbane in the State of Queensland*, 1934, 'Letitia Jane Atherton', Mackay, The Government.

[99] Clark, Betty, 1992, *A House Well Filled*, Mackay, Mackay Printing & Publishing, p.24.

At the time of Letitia's retirement in 1914, the family had sold their northern properties and went to live at Yeerongpilly.[100] Letitia and Richard were parents to Vida Althea as previously mentioned, who married Albert Alfred Cook and an entry for Vida can be found later in this book. Atherton died in Brisbane at the age of 85 at the home of her son Aubrey, and was buried in Dutton Park Cemetery, eight years after the death of her husband Richard.[101]

Events:

- 1868 Arrived in Brisbane, Australia
- 1870 Arrived in the Mackay district ten years after the area was first settled by Europeans
- 1914 The Athertons relocated to Brisbane

Figure 6 Letitia Jane Orr. Photograph courtesy of Craig Derek Bainbridge.

---

[100] Obituaries Australia, 2024, *Richard Atherton (1847-1926)*, viewed 1/5/2024, https://oa.anu.edu.au/obituary/atherton-richard-22361

[101] Deaths, 'Atherton', 1834, *The Courier-Mail*, Monday 9 April, p.10. viewed 20/04/2024 http://nal/gov/au/nla.news-article1187594

Azar, Mary (1876-1957)

Figure 7 A drawing of the Ambassador Hotel built by Mary Azar in 1937. Photograph courtesy of Sugar City Art Deco and Modernisation Society.

Born:
- 1876
- Bicheri, Lebanon

Died:
- 23 March 1957
- Nudgee Cemetery and Cremitorium, Nudgee, Brisbane, Queensland.

Occupation:
- Hotellier and businesswoman. Azar successfully managed a hotel which she designed and built in the art décor style that remains as a functioning hotel today.

Alternative Name/s:
- Mary Catha-Ketter-Cutter-Cutler-Hatter[102]

---

[102] Mary Azar's family name is Catha for her birth details, Cutter or Hatta or Cutler on electoral rolls and Ketter on cemetery records.

Summary:

Mary Catha was born in 1876 in Bicheri or Bicchieri, (named after a family or location) in Lebanon to Joseph and Paoli Catha. Little is known of her parents or siblings. Catha at 19 years married Elias Azar aged 35 years, in Atherton, North Queensland on 23 January 1895. She lived in Queensland for sixty-three years.[103] Elias Azar was of Syrian origin and arrived in Australia from the United States in 1885.[104]

They had twelve children. Susan born 1896 (married Joseph Peter Abdullah in 1915); Josephine born 1897 (married John Michael Moses in 1905); George born 1900; Alice born 1902 (married Walter Alexandra Flegler in 1925; Michael born 1903; John born 1905; Elsie Marion born 1908 (married John Clifton Wilson in 1935); Alexander born 1910; Esme Phyllis born 1913; Thomas Vincent born 1916; Augustine Bernard born 1918; and Mavis Joyce born 1922.

The Azars began their career in Atherton, North Queensland. Mary worked as a saleswoman and Elias as a hawker, prior to starting their thirty-year draper's business. In the 1920s the family purchased a property at Yattee, just south of Cairns. Elias died at their home in Brisbane in 1928 leaving his wife with three small children. Mavis, the youngest, was just 6 years old. After he died, Azar travelled to Tully where her older children lived and onto Yeppoon before moving to Mackay.

Azar was hotelkeeper of Tattersalls Hotel in 1936, and her daughter Esme Phyllis was the manageress in 1937. Her son Michael worked as a barman at the Commercial Hotel in Mackay.[105] Females as hoteliers was not uncommon in the early

---

[103] *Death in the District of Brisbane in the State of Queensland*, 1957, 'Mary Azar', Brisbane, The Government.
[104] Bowden, Vicky, 2021, 'Mackay History: Ambassador Hotel Rises from Tattersalls Ashes', *The Courier Mail,* 2 September, viewed 15 January 2023, https://www.couriermail.com.au
[105] Australian Electoral Commission, 1937, *Australia Electoral Rolls*, 1903-1980, Canberra, AEC, viewed 2023-01-20, http://www.ancestry.com.au

days. Up until the 1860s, publicans were expected to live on the premises and provide meals and accommodation. Women as the carers in the family often had to provide for dependents and domestic work was very familiar to them.

Just prior to moving into the recently purchased timber hotel, it caught fire and was reduced to ashes. Fortunately, the hotel was insured, so plans went ahead to rebuild the over 60-year-old timber structure that had survived severe damage during the 1918 cyclone.[106] Azar sold off what could be salvaged from the burnt-out building by auction. It was reported that she paid £14,500 for the new build a larger sum than the insurance payout for the old Tattersalls premises. Esme Phyllis Azar changed the name of the hotel from the Tattersalls Hotel to the Ambassador Hotel in December of 1936. [107]

The Ambassador Hotel was built by William Guthrie noted for his famed Art Deco style of buildings in 1937. The architect was J G (Joseph) Rooney of Townsville. Various local sub-contractors in Mackay completed the fixtures and fittings. The building was known for its striking frontal appearance. It was built entirely of reinforced concrete, making it fireproof. Once completed, the hotel offered accommodation (with hot and cold running water at 17 shillings per day) and a venue for gatherings. Guests entered the hotel through a palm-lined porch protected by artistically wrought iron gates. The hotel offered a sound-proof telephone booth, with booking office and waiting room at the end of the hall. A highlight was the mammoth oval-shaped island bar that occupied the central floor space surrounded by a terrazzo marble footrest with glazed tile sides. Electric chandeliers and fans provided light and ventilation. Large lead-light panels along the walls also added light. Many other attractive features impressed

---

[106] 'The Cyclone at Mackay: A detailed Report', 1918, *Morning Bulletin*, Tuesday 29 January, p.6., viewed 2023-01-20 http://nla.gov.au/nla.news-article53836066
[107] 'Two Applications Refused: Licensing Commission', 1936, *Courier-Mail*, Saturday 12 December, p.13. viewed 2023-01-17 https://nla.gov.au

visitors to this new hotel.[108] The hotel now offers dining-in and take-away food, a bar, venues for parties, events, functions amidst stunning river views.

Azar hosted the wedding reception for her second youngest daughter, Esme Phyllis who married John Reginald Hurley in May of 1937. The reception took place at the new Ambassador Hotel following their marriage at St Patrick's Roman Catholic Church in Mackay. Michael Azar gave the bride away as her father was deceased. The bride wore an ivory hammered satin gown exquisitely shirred in silver from the neckline to the hem. This elaborate dress was matched with a Limerick lace veil and a bouquet of eucharis lilies, lilies of the valley and maiden hair fern.[109]

The life of a hotelier was not just one of celebrations. Later that year, proceedings were taken out against Azar for allegedly selling drinks after 12 am. It was explained that the bar had closed earlier that night, but a few patrons had requested one last drink before leaving. A policeman entered the hotel at 12 am just as drinks were served. The defendant's representative pleaded guilty on her behalf, and she was fined ten pounds and six shillings costs. The four drinkers were fined ten shillings each, also with six shillings costs[110]

The Azars were only managing the Ambassador Hotel for a brief period before they returned to Brisbane. It was sold in November 1938, twelve months after being built, to J H (John) Thompson for the substantial sum of £24,000 - - a healthy return of £14,500 on the investment. It sold again in 1951 for a record price of £42,500 to Joseph Edward Jackson, licensee of the Railway Hotel.[111]

---

[108] 'Hotel Ambassador: Fine Modern Residential Opening Function To-Night', 1937, *Daily Mercury*, 3 September, p.13, viewed 2023-01-17 http://nla.gov.au.
[109] 'Sunday Wedding Growing Popular', 1938, *Telegraph*, Saturday 28 May, p.13, viewed 2023-01-17 http://nla.gov.au
[110] 'Licensing Court: Actions Against Licensee', 1938, *Daily Mercury*, Saturday 20 August, p.12, viewed 2023-01-22 http://nla.gov.au
[111] 'Freehold Record', 1951, *Daily Mercury*, Friday 26 January, p.2., viewed 2023-01-23 http://nla.gov.au

As a mother, Azar knew the stress and anxiety of seeing her children go to war. Five of her sons joined the armed services during the Second World War. Joseph joined the Australian Military Forces in May of 1940.[112] Augustine Bernard, a public accountant, joined in May of 1941.[113] John, was a draper, married at the time of enlistment and joined the Australian Military Forces in June of 1942.[114] Michael joined in August of 1942 [115] as did Alexander.[116] All her sons returned home from the war although at least two of them suffered with ill health.

Azar moved back to her home in Brisbane after the sale of the hotel. Her son Michael who was a host at the Ambassador Hotel left for Brisbane after two and a half years in Mackay.[117] Azar was living at Greenslopes in 1954 and died in Brisbane in 1957. She is buried beside her husband Elias in Nudgee Cemetery.

Events:

- 1896 Draper's business, Atherton, North Queensland
- 1937 Purchased Tattersalls Hotel, Mackay Queensland
- 1937 Built the Art deco Ambassador Hotel
- 1938 Sold the Ambassador Hotel
- 1939 Moved to Brisbane

---

[112] National Archives of Australia, 1940, *Azar Joseph: Service Number QX4913*, Cairns, NAA, viewed 2023-01-16 https://recordsearch.naa.gov.au

[113] National Archives of Australia, 1941, *Azar Augustine Bernard, Service Number Q90034*, Brisbane, NAA. Viewed 2023-01-15 https://recordsearch.naa.gov.au

[114] National Archives of Australia, 1942, *Azar John: Service Number Q209866*, Proston, Qld, NAA, viewed 2023-01-15 https://recordsexrch.naa.gov.au

[115] National Archives of Australia, 1942, *Azar Michael: Service Number Q209369*, Proston, Qld, NAA, viewed 2023-01-15 https://recordsexrch.naa.gov.au

[116] National Archives of Australia, 1942, *Azar Alexander: Service Number QX51494*, Proston, Qld, NAA, viewed 2023-01-15 https://recordsexrch.naa.gov.au

[117] 'Personal', 1939, *Daily Mercury*, Friday 3 February, p.8., viewed 2023-01-21 http://nla.gov.au

Figure 8 Advertisement placed in the *Daily Mercury* Friday 15 Oct. 1937 p.12.

Barlow, Grace Elizabeth, Matron (1884-1972)

Figure 9 Matron Barlow and staff at Ormond Private Hospital, Mackay. Photograph taken in 1912. Courtesy of Glenys Kyle.

Born:
- 1884
- Islington, London, England

Died:
- 30 April 1972
- Mackay, Queensland

Occupation:
- Matron, Ormond Private Hospital. Barlow also worked at the Mackay District Hospital during war time and once married, provided medical assistance as a private citizen, to those in need.

Alternative Name/s:
- Grace Elizabeth Christensen, Grace Barlon

Summary:

Grace Barlow, second daughter of Walter Alfred Barlow (a chorister at St Pauls, London) and Elizabeth Sarah Butwell, was born in 1884, and baptised on 1 February 1885 at the Church of St Mary, Islington, and London. Due to health reasons, (possibly bronchitis), at the age of 16 she departed from London aboard the steamship *Jumna,* and on 22 September 1900, arrived in Brisbane, seventy-five days later.[118] It could be speculated that the State of Queensland needed nursing staff or at least marriageable aged women as there were 287 female immigrants (some hospital trained nurses) aboard the *Jumna* under the supervision of a matron and a sub-matron.

Upon arrival in Brisbane, an inquiry was undertaken into the behaviour of some of the immigrants (unnamed), the matron/s, surgeons, and other staff during and after the voyage, by the Board of Immigration at Kangaroo Point, Brisbane. The alleged behaviour was that some of the girls made appointments with males during the day and kept the appointments at night, and at least one girl was intoxicated after arrival in Brisbane. It was also alleged that the Matron was reputed to be 'harsh' on the girls for their behaviour. The outcome of the inquiry was not conclusive in its findings.[119]

Another record indicates that a Grace Barlon travelled to Australia in December 1900 on the *Duke of Norfolk*, although the entry in the passenger list has a line drawn through it, which could indicate a cancelled passage.[120] She travelled as a domestic servant.

Barlow trained as a nurse at the Children's Hospital, Brisbane and won the Ambulance Medallion. She completed a St John Ambulance Association Home Nursing Certificate in 1902 at the Brisbane Technical College.[121] This qualification was further

---

[118] 'Schedule B: Form of Passenger List', *Jumna*, 1900, *Ancestry.com*, viewed 19/09/2023, http://ancestry.com

[119] *Brisbane Courier*, 1900, Tuesday 27 November. P.8., and Monday 3 December, p.9., viewed 17 September 2023 http://nla.gov.au

[120] 'Schedule B: Form of Passenger List', *Duke of Norfolk*, 1900, Ancestry.com, viewed 19/09/2023, http://ancestry.com

[121] 'St John Ambulance Certificates', 1902, *Brisbane Courier*, Tuesday 28 October, p.4., viewed 19/09/2023, http://nla.gov.au/nla.news-article19199989

added to with a St John Ambulance First Aid Certificate in 1905[122] and a First Aid in the Wounded Certificate in 1906.[123]

Barlow's nursing career was underway in 1908, with Australian Electoral records indicating that she had worked as a nurse at the Children's Hospital, Ithaca, a Brisbane suburb.[124] She had also worked at the Children's Sanatorium, Sandgate. In 1911 through to 1913, she was appointed matron at Dr Williams's private hospital, (known as Ormond Hospital) Mackay.[125] Following this appointment she also worked for a time as matron at the Mackay District Hospital, relieving Matron Langford who enlisted in the First World War.[126]

The Ormond hospital was designed by Dr Williams, consisting of two high-set buildings with wide verandahs roofed in bull nosed iron and enclosed by wooden-laced balustrades and latticed panels. The building was described as reflecting an Edwardian elegance. In May 1911, patients were admitted with medical surgical and maternity cases.[127] The hospital was fitted out with the latest medical equipment of those times. Dr Williams sold the property in 1919 to the Ivers sisters. Following a conversation between Dr Charles Emmanuel Williams and Father (later Monsignor) Joseph Mulcahy during a game of bowls on the City Bowling Club green, it was decided that the Ormond Hospital would make an ideal new medical complex. It later became the Mackay Mater Misericordiae Hospital in 1927. Since that time, the Mater Hospital site was rebuilt as a complex of shops and a supermarket in 1987.[128]

---

[122] 'St John Ambulance Association', 1905, *Brisbane Courier*, Tuesday 25 July, p.4., viewed 19/09/2023 http://nla.gov.au/nla-news-article19312601

[123] 'Expert in First Aid', 1906, *Telegraph*, Saturday 4 August, p.3., viewed 19/09/2023 http://nla.gov.au/nla-news-article175093008

[124] Barlow, Grace, 1908, Division of Brisbane: Subdivision of Ithaca, *Australian Electoral Commission*, viewed 19/09/2023, http://ancestry.com

[125] 'New Private Hospital', 1911, *Daily Mercury*, Friday 12 May, p.6., viewed 19/09/2023, http://nla.gov.au/nla.news-article172443341

[126] ibid., *p.4-5*. 1927-1987,

[127] ibid. pp.4-5.

[128] Wright, Bernice, 1987, *Mater Hospital Mackay 1927-1987*, Mackay, Qld., Mercury Printing Services, p.4.

Long before then, Matron Barlow married a Homebush man, Albert Bendix Christensen; - the youngest child of Ingwert and Maran Christensen - who was eight years her junior, on 14 April 1915. The couple never had children.[129] It may have been that the 'marriage bar' was the reason that Matron Barlow no longer worked in a professional capacity after marriage. The choice was between giving up their professional career and or hiding the fact that they had married which would have been difficult for someone who held a prominent position in a small community such as Mackay in 1915. The 'marriage bar' in the Australian Public Service was not abolished until 1966.[130]

For whatever reason, Christensen retired from a professional nursing career, living at first with her husband in Albert Street, Mackay when he worked as a sugar boiler. In 1921, she moved with him when he worked as an alluvial tin miner at Mount Spurgeon, about 18 km from Mossman. Mossman is located about 76 km north of Cairns in North Queensland. In 1930, they were recorded as living at Louisa Creek via Alligator Creek, much closer to Mackay, and in 1932, they were living on a cane farm at Fernvale, Kungurri, near Dows Creek about 50 km west of Mackay. They lived at this farm for a considerable number of years until they retired to Louisa Creek.[131]

It was during the years they were living at Kungurri that Christensen again performed nursing duties to the local community. A letter written by Christensen to the *Daily Mercury*, expressed concern about previous published suggestions for the treatment of a stonefish bite. Detailed comments and treatment were given. People were warned that the stonefish are common in freshwater creeks as well as the ocean. Her advice was that if the bites are treated correctly and promptly then a full recovery could be expected in

---

[129] *Death in the District of Mackay in the State of Queensland*, 1972, 'Grace Elizabeth Christensen', Mackay, The Government.

[130] Crabb, Annabel, 2016, 'The Forgotten Milestone that Shows How Far Australian Women Have Come', viewed 19/09/2023 https://www.smh.com/au

[131] Australian Electoral Commission, 1906-1970, *Electoral Roll*, Canberra, AEC, viewed 19/09/2023 https://ancestry.com

a few hours. The letter was signed by her with the designation of Member of the Australian Teaching Nurses Association (MATNA).[132] A distant relative of Christensen comments that for the many years the couple lived at Kungurri; Christensen provided much needed first aid in the area. She attended various accidents in the days when people drove a horse and sulky as well as writing many letters to the Editor of the *Daily Mercury*.[133] It could be speculated as to what her career would have been like if she had continued her nursing career after marriage.

Christensen lived for seventy-two years in Queensland and died at the age of 88 years. She was married for 55 years when her husband died. Her burial took place alongside her husband at Mount Bassett Cemetery, Mackay.

Events:

- 1900 Arrived in Australia
- 1911 Matron Ormond Private Hospital, Mackay
- 1914 Matron Mackay District Hospital
- 1915 Married Albert Bendix Christensen

Figure 10 Ormond Private Hospital, at the corner of formerly Albert now Gordon and Brisbane Streets, Mackay. Photograph courtesy of the Sisters of Mercy Archives, Rockhampton.

---

[132] Christensen, Grace E., 193?, *Daily Mercury*, 9 May, *Facebook*, viewed 19/09/2023. Courtesy of Glenys Kyle.
[133] Kyle, Glenys, *Facebook*, viewed 22/09/2023 https://www.facebook.com/search/top/?q=Matron%20Barlow

Berry, Dr Annie Hayes (Nan) (1912-1998) OBE

Figure 11 Standing: B Griffiths, M Armstrong, R McBride Sitting: M Riley, Nan Berry, (Head) J Foley. 1931 Prefects. Wellington Girls College, New Zealand. Photograph courtesy of WGC.

Born:
- 6 Jul 1912
- Carterton, Wellington, New Zealand.

Died:
- 17 Jan 1998
- Martinborough Cemetery, Martinborough, South Wairarapa District, Wellington, New Zealand.

Occupation:
- The first and only female surgeon, and superintendent at the Mackay Base Hospital. Dr Berry was an all-time favourite with the Mackay public. She was awarded the Officer of the Order of the British Empire (OBE) for meritorious service to the citizens of Mackay.

Alternative Name/s
- 'Nan' Berry as she was known at Wellington Girls College. Dr Berry.

Summary:

Dr Annie Hayes Berry, the first and only woman to hold the position of Medical and Surgical Superintendent of Mackay Base Hospital, was born in 1912 in New Zealand. Her parents were Joseph Smith Berry, and her mother was Aileen (Powell) Berry. Dr Berry had a sister, Aileen Joan Berry (1914-1991).[134]

Dr Annie Berry was educated firstly by correspondence before attending Lyttleton High School and Wellington Girls College (WGC) followed by attending the University of Otago. During her college years, Annie Berry won awards and prizes: in 1928 she was the winner of the Mary Izard memorial prize; first and second in most subjects in 1929; prefect; Junior Red Cross and captain of the winning team of the Home Nursing Competition; first and second in Home Science and history in 1930. She was head prefect in 1931; president of Junior Red Cross; member of many committees; first prize in the Rangiriri Original prose competition; Dux of School; and won many other prizes. She gained a Higher Leaving Certificate. Berry was a high achiever and was fully involved in school life. The WGC showed that she went on to study medicine at the University of Otago.[135]

She graduated in 1937 and travelled to Australia, working in hospitals in Melbourne, Sydney and Adelaide before serving in Innisfail, North Queensland.

Dr Berry worked at the Mackay District Hospital in June 1942, shortly after the Battle of the Coral Sea. Her legendary compassion for the sick and wounded servicemen in her care during World War II (WWII) was reflected in the high regard that was held by the ex-servicemen throughout her medical career. She was honoured by the Returned Servicemen's League (RSL) for her work during the war.

---

[134] 'Annie Hayes Berry', 2023, viewed 2023-01-12 https://ancestry.com
[135] Vhairi Miles, 2023, Wellington Girls College, New Zealand, email January 30, vhairi.miles@wgc.school.nz

Dr Berry was appointed Acting Superintendent at Mackay Base Hospital in July 1944. She was well loved by the Mackay community and when, at the end of WW II, she was told her term in Mackay was over, a public outcry resulted in the Queensland Department of Health's reversing its decision. She was appointed Medial Superintendent in 1946, possibly the first woman superintendent of a large general hospital in Australia or New Zealand.[136]

Though regarded as a disciplinarian, Dr Berry was always loyal to her staff, and the staff returned that loyalty. This was born out in the long service of many staff members. She excelled at reigning in spending and thus was of great assistance to the hospital's administration. She led by example with her high standard of professionalism and care, and yet, in her self-effacing manner, she said on her retirement, 'I may have been the conductor of the band, but I only made a little noise myself.'[137] A tireless worker, she often spent all night administering to a critically ill patient. In 1964, she was awarded the Officer of the Order of the British Empire (OBE) for meritorious service to the citizens of Mackay.[138]

On her retirement in October 1972, tributes were made for her long-standing contribution to the Mackay community, to ex-servicemen and to the Aboriginal and Islander communities. She returned to her mother's former home at Island Bay, New Zealand where she grew up. She died in Wellington in 1998, aged 85.

Dr Berry was an important figure in the transition to modern medicine in Mackay. She held a top executive position in a man's world, yet she maintained her dignity and earned the highest respect of men and women alike. A ward at the Mackay Base Hospital, built during her time as superintendent, carriers her name. She deserves to be remembered for her leadership role in medicine in Mackay.

---

[136] Mackay Family History Society, 2012, 'Annie Berry', Mackay, The Society.
[137] 'New Year's Honours: Knighthoods for 13 Australians', 1964, *Canberra Times*, Wednesday 1 January, p.1-2, viewed 2023-01-10 https://nla.gov.au
[138] ibid.

Events:

- 1928-1931 Wellington Girls College, New Zealand
- 1931-1937 University of Otago, New Zealand
- 1944 Acting Superintendent Mackey Base Hospital
- 1946 Superintendent Mackay Base Hospital
- 1972 Retired to New Zealand

Awards:

- 1964 Officer of the Order of the British Empire (OBE)

Figure 12 Dr Berry and staff at the Mackay District Hospital. Photograph courtesy of *Facebook*.com

Cook, Dorothy Berris (1909-1995)

Figure 13 Dorothy Berris Drysdale Cook on her wedding day in 1950. Photograph courtesy of *The Courier Mail*.

Born:
- 21 October 1909
- Brisbane, Queensland

Died:
- 1 July 1995
- Mackay District

Occupation:
- Philanthropist, socialite, businesswoman, grazier, and musician. Cook was the centre of Mackay society for many years and donated her wealth back to the Mackay community when she died.

Alternative Name/s
- Dorothy Berris Drysdale, Dorothy Berris Cook, Dorothy Cook,
- "The last Lady of Greenmount'

Summary:

Dorothy Drysdale was the eldest daughter of Malcolm Lauchlan Drysdale and Hannah Davies. Dorothy was born on the same day and just before her identical twin Olwyn Sybil Drysdale.[139] Drysdale was the great niece of John Drysdale, a pioneering family of the Burdekin sugar industry. She was also related to the eminent Australian artist Sir George Russell Drysdale. The Drysdale's youngest daughter was Gwendolin Ellen born in 1914.[140] Gwendolin married John Owen Amos in 1936 and had a daughter Judith Ann Amos. Gwendolin died young at the age of 28.

George Drysdale, great grandfather to Dorothy, came to Australia from Kirkholm, Wigtownshire, Scotland in 1862 aboard the sailing ship *Conway*[141] with his wife Matilda, son James and daughter Ann.[142] The family name in Scotland which can be traced back to the 16th century, was changed from Douglas to Drysdale after a skirmish with the neighbours that resulted in the deaths of three of them. Therefore, Drysdale was the adopted name of the Douglas family, taken from the local parish church. George Drysdale's occupation on arrival in Australia was listed as a farmer. They settled and grew their family at Coomera on the Gold Coast. Malcolm Drysdale's father was born to Ann Bratton Drysdale a daughter of George Drysdale. Ann Bratton was 17 years old when her son Malcolm was born. His father's name remained unknown. Malcolm adopted his grandfather's surname of Drysdale even though his mother married Peter Yaun, a Scottish immigrant and carpenter in 1894.

---

[139] 'Generosity Marked Woman's Life', 1995, *The Daily Mercury*, Thursday July 6, p.5.

[140] Clark, Betty, 1992, *A House Well Filled*, Mackay, Mackay Printing & Publishing, p121.

[141] Bowden, Vicky, 2020, 'Mackay History: The Last lady of Greenmount Homestead', *The Courier Mail*, October 1, viewed 15/03/2024 https://www.couriermail.com.au/news/queensland/mackay/mackay-history-

[142] 'Assisted Immigration 1848-1912', 1862, *Queensland State Archives*, 27 November 1862, viewed 15/03/2024 https://www.archivessearch.qld.gov.au/api/download_file/DR38087

Bratton subsequently had twin sons (Roderik and Ronald) with Yuan in 1900 when she was aged 34. The twins were half-brothers to Malcolm, born when he was 22 years old.[143] Malcolm married Dorothy's mother Hannah Davies in Brisbane in January of 1908 when he was 30 and Davies was 25.[144] His occupation was recorded as a labourer on electoral rolls although the *Australian City Directories 1845-1948* lists him as a storekeeper in Coomera in 1918. Malcolm died in 1941 at the age of 63.

Both the Drysdale's were successful at music examinations held by Trinity College, Dalby, in 1923 and passed examinations to attend the state high school in 1925.[145] Both sisters were successful in religious studies[146] and music examinations held at Trinity College, Dalby in 1923.[147] Their younger sister Gwen was prominent in the Dalby School of Arts Maypole dance when the twins featured in a performance, singing a Japanese song.[148] The twins also featured in many social events as they were growing up in particular the Debutante Ball held on France's National Day in 1930, at Rowe's Banqueting Hall, Brisbane.[149]

Drysdale was educated at the Clayfield Ladies' College in Brisbane and entered a business partnership with her mother and sister, Olwyn, as 'dressmakers and milliners.'[150] Her maternal grandfather, Joshua Davies had been a tailor in Cardigan, Wales, United Kingdom.[151] The business was a lady's dress shop by the name of 'Nanette' in Brisbane possibly profiting from skills

---

[143] Bowden, Vicky, op. cit.
[144] ibid.
[145] 'High School: 1906 Candidates', 1925, *Daily Mail*, Saturday 10 January, p.12. viewed 24/03/2024 http://nla.gov.au/nla.news-article218334222
[146] 'Sunday School Examinations', 1922, *Dalby Herald*, Tuesday 3 October, p.2., viewed 24/03/2024 http://nla.gov.au/nla.news-article215442398
[147] 'Dalby', 1923, *Toowoomba Chronicle and Darling Downs Gazette,* Thursday 26 July, p.2., viewed 24/03/2024 http://nla.gov.au/nla.news=article253721777
[148] ibid.
[149] 'Alliance Francaise', 1930, *Brisbane Courier*, Tuesday 15 July p.18. viewed 24/03/2024 http://nla.gov.au/nla.news-article21541715
[150] Generosity Marked Woman's Life, op. cit. p.1.
[151] Bowden, Vicky, op. cit.

passed on by their grandfather and business skills from their father. Olwyn died at the relatively young age of 52 after marrying in 1933, divorcing, remarrying and then separating - Dorothy was engaged briefly in 1944.

Their business continued until after Drysdale's wedding in January 1950 to Thomas Albert Cook. Following their engagement in November of 1949,[152] the lead up to her marriage was a hectic one for Drysdale to be fitting other brides for weddings and then organising her own.[153]

Thomas (Tom) Albert Cook of Greenmount, Mackay was the eldest and only remaining son of Albert Alfred Cook (1875-1948) and Vida Althea Atherton (1875-1955). Albert Cook was the son of early settlers in the Mackay district, John Cook (1838-1901) and Elizabeth Cormack Ross (1838-1907). Greenmount Homestead was built by Albert Cook for his wife Vida in 1915 on land that the founder of Mackay, (John Mackay) had settled in 1862.[154] The marriage of Drysdale and Cook was the joining of two families who settled early in Queensland, the Drysdales had interests centering around the Pioneer and Inkerman Mills, while the Cook family were among the first settlers in the Mackay district.

Greenmount Homestead was reportedly built 200 feet above sea level and gives sweeping views across the Mackay district. The home, decorated and furnished in the 1950s style, has wide verandahs to facilitate a breeze, an entrance hall, four bedrooms as well as an area where Hannah Drysdale lived and at times where the visiting Governor stayed. There was also an office, library, kitchen, laundry and staff quarters attached to the main house. Gloria Arrow previously mentioned in an earlier entry was a domestic servant of the Cooks. The Homestead is now a local museum containing records and artefacts of the Cook dynasty.

---

[152] 'Faces and places', 1949, *Queensland Country Life*, Thursday 17 November, p.7., viewed 27/03/2024 http://nla.gov.au/nla.news-article97120519
[153] ibid.
[154] Clark, Betty, op. cit., pp. 73-75.

Dorothy and Tom Cook were married on 30 January 1950 at St John's Cathedral, Brisbane. The elegantly dressed bride wore a handmade Brussels lace veil loaned for the occasion.[155] Her attendants were her twin sister Olwyn Thomas and Tom's sister Althea Cook. Both wore gowns of gleaming French lame made in a Victorian style. Walter Beatty and Harvey Graham attended the bridegroom. Following an extended honeymoon in Sydney, Melbourne and Hobart, the couple began their life at Greenmount Homestead in Mackay. The groom's mother and sister having moved out of the family home went to live at Sea Brae, Bucasia, the beach retreat built by Albert and Vida Cook. Cook was 41 years old at the time of her marriage and Tom was 40. They appeared to be a happily married couple for thirty-one years although the couple were childless.[156]

The couple lived modestly at Greenmount. Cook's requests to Tom, prior to her marriage were modest, those of a new bedroom suite, an updated bathroom to accommodate a bath and an Aga stove.[157] Cook busied herself with membership to the Women's Guild of Walkerston Anglican Church and Meals on Wheels.[158]

When visiting her mother following her marriage, Cook stayed at the *Canberra Hotel* in Brisbane.[159] The Cook's social life in

---

[155] 'Married Last Night: Bride Wore Handmade Lace Veil', 1950, *The Courier Mail*, Wednesday 1 February, viewed 27/03/2024 http://nla/gov/au/nla.news-article49718266

[156] ibid.

[157] Gcasandra, 2018, '10 Pioneering Women Who Shaped Mackay's Future', March 3, *The Courier Mail*, viewed 27/03/2023 https://www.couriermail.com.au/news/queensland/mackay/10-poineering women-who-shaped-Mackay's-future

[158] Clark, Betty, op. cit., p.123.

[159] The Canberra Hotel was situated on the corner of Ann and Edward Streets, opposite the Salvation Army's People's Palace. It was built in 1929 by the Queensland Prohibition League and later owned by the Temperance League. Its aim was to provide accommodation in an alcohol-free environment. It was known as the 'City Hotel for country people'. The building was subsequently replaced by the Mincom building. State Library Queensland, 2012, 'Sobriety in Ruins: Demolition of The Canberra Hotel', viewed 24/03/2024 https://www.slq.qld.gov.au/blog/sobriety-ruins-demolition-canberra-hotel

Mackay expanded with various social events including the visits of the Governor of Queensland, Sir Henry Abel Smith and his wife, Lady May in 1962, whose photographs reside in the homestead.[160] The British High Commissioner was also another notable visitor to the property. Garden parties, farewells and fashion shows were often held with many of the female staff modelling women's clothes. The Cooks benefitted from the foresight and investment of both John Cook who settled at Balnagowan and Albert Alfred Cook who purchased the land and built Greanmount Homestead.

Investments were those of share in Pleystowe Mill and the shares purchased by Tom Cook in the Mackay Steam Laundry. The Cooks were involved with the Mackay Turf Club, The Mackay Historical Society and Museum and many other charitable organisations. Cook also assisted her husband in an exotic breeding program by introducing the Brangus, Santa Gertrudis stud and other breeds of cattle to the property.

The couple bought a property at Buderim, on the Sunshine Coast north of Brisbane in 1975 from where they made occasional visits to Mackay. During this time, Cook was hospitalised for a serious nervous disorder resulting in her husband spending many years supporting his wife through her illness. It was in 1981 that Tom became ill and died in November of that year.[161]

Following the death of her husband, Cook's health limited her community activities, but she was able to distribute a considerable amount of funds to many worthy charities. International, national and local institutions benefitted from her generosity. An amount of nearly two million dollars was donated to notable causes namely the Royal Flying Doctor Service, the Royal Blind Society, the Leukemia Foundation, UNICEF, World Vision, Austcare, Blue Nursing, Queensland Cancer Foundation, Heart Foundation, Asthma Australia, Mackay Art Society, Mackay

---

[160] Mackay Regional Council, 2024, 'Welcome to Greenmount Homestead: Self-Guided Tour', [booklet] viewed 24/03/2024 https://www.mackay.qld.gov.au/facilities/parks_and_projects/park_weddings/greenmount_homestead

[161] 'Generosity Marked Woman's Life', op. cit. p.5.

Legacy, Crossroads, Brisbane City Mission, The Salvation Army Appeal, Lifeline and Aged Persons' Homes to mention a few. Major donations were made to Australian Rotary Health Research Foundation and Rotary awarded both a Paul Harris fellowship and a Companion on Australian Rotary Health Research in different years in recognition of Cook's generosity. She also funded a library at the Central Queensland University, Mackay Campus. The building was named the Hannah Drysdale Library in honour of her mother.[162] The Cooks gifted their home to the Mackay Regional Council (now known as Greenmount Historic Homestead and the 'Tom and Dorothy Memorial Park'), for use by the community, researchers and visitors. The contents of the home were donated to the Mackay Historical Society. Cook also founded a Resource Centre, built on the property, which displays memorabilia other than that pertaining to the Cook family[163] as well as many of the Cooks family history records.

Her final gift was that of research scholarships offered at James Cook University in Townsville. The scholarships are offered to research students undertaking a Master or Doctor of Philosophy in the field of public health, laboratory and clinical investigation of population health in tropical North Queensland, with a focus on the Mackay and Central Queensland region.[164] As the Cooks did not have children, it would seem that Cook took a particular interest in the welfare of her staff especially Gloria Arrow who had been an employee for many years. A book about Arroww's life was published.[165] Arrow believed that the Cooks particularly Dorothy, had treated her as a daughter. As a childless person of some means, Cook may have had a greater interest in providing financially for the local community by way of generous donations and funding of research scholarships.

---

[162] Wilson, Geoff, 1992, *University of Central Queensland*, June 30, p.1. Letter received addressed to Mrs D Cook on the June 30, 1992, Greenmount Historic Homestead Archives.
[163] ibid., p.5.
[164] 'Tom and Dorothy Cook Scholarships in Public Health and Tropical Medicine', 2024, viewed 24/03/2024 http://www.jcu.edu.au/b/scholarships/search/tom-and-dorothy-cook...
[165] Smith, Jan, 1998, *The Dark Daughter: A Mackay Story*, Mackay, Quick Printers.

Cook had suffered poor health and depression over many years and died peacefully at Kawana Waters Nursing Home, Caloundra on 1 July 1995 aged 85. She was buried at Walkerston Cemetery, near Mackay. Her death ended the enormous contribution she and her husband had made to the history of North Queensland and Queenslanders. Arrow, who had worked in a domestic capacity for the Cooks since she was a young woman, became a tour guide and caretaker of the homestead until her passing in 2021.[166]

Events:

- 1950 Dorothy married Tom Cook and resided in Mackay
- 1962 Visit by Governor of Queensland, Sir Henry Abel Smith and his wife, Lady May
- 1975 The Cooks moved to Buderim
- 1981 Dorothy Cook returned to Mackay to settle financial affairs following the death of her husband Tom Cook

Links:

Greenmount Historic Homestead: https://www.mackay.qld.gov.au/facilities/council_facilities/historical_centres/greenmount_homestead

Figure 14 Greenmount Historic Homestead. Photograph courtesy of Mackay Regional Council.

---

[166] Miko, Tara, 2021, Tributes Flow for Greenmount Homestead's Former Caretaker Gloria Arrow', *The Courier Mail*, viewed 3/05/2024 https://www.couriermail.com.au/news/queensland/mackay/tributes-flow-for-greenmount-homesteads-former-caretaker-gloria-arrow/news-story/08fccc71f733347b4522bed7568c3b89

Cook, Elizabeth Cormack Ross (1838-1907)

Figure 15 Elizabeth Cormack Ross Cook. Photograph courtesy of Greenmount Historic Homestead Collection.

Born:
- 21 October 1838
- Kilmuir Easter, Ross and Cromarty, Ross-shire, Scotland

Died:
- 24 February 1907
- Balnagowan, Mackay District

Occupation:
- Grazier. Ross was born into a grazing family and combined her family's wealth with that of the Cooks to create a dynasty in the Mackay region.

Alternative Name/s
- 'Lizzie', Elizabeth Cook, Elizabeth Cormack Ross

Summary:

Elizabeth Ross was the daughter of Robert Ross, a surveyor, and Margaret Sutherland of Ross-shire in Scotland. She had two brothers and a sister; Louis Gerald Ross, who sponsored her voyage to Australia for the cost of £7 in 1856; Alexander, her younger brother; and an older sister Ann Cormack Ross. Louis Gerald Ross arrived in July of 1852[167] aboard the *Maria Somes* and died in Queensland in March of 1870.[168] Ross was 22 years of age when she arrived in Australia. The Ross and Cook families were graziers in the Armidale district of northern New South Wales (NSW) and would have known of each other's families.

Ross married John Cook in 1860. John was born at Turanville, Scone, NSW on 3 April 1838. His parents were Samuel Wellington Cook (1803-1883), and his mother was Elizabeth Cary Dangar (1805-1978). Their first daughter Florence Elizabeth Cary Cormack Cook Reid was born at Nemingha NSW in 1861 and died 16 May 1924. Two further children quickly followed, Alexandria Sutherland Ross Cook born in 1863 who died in 1867, and Samuel William Wellington Cook was born in 1865 and died in 1933. During this time, her husband was establishing properties in Queensland with Louis Gerald Ross, his brother-in-law, and was away much of the time - a difficulty many young women encountered when immigrating to Australia.

Brother of Elizabeth, Louis G Ross was made aware by John Mackay returning south following his explorations, of the potential to purchase land near Mackay in Queensland. Ross then leased land near Mackay and named it Balnagowan after his Scottish ancestral home. Prior to this, he had entered into an agreement with John Cook (Elizabeth's husband) whereby the two men were to have an equal share in any land taken up. Following his drowning in 1870, when he tried to swim a flooded river, there was a dispute amongst the Ross family about ownership of the property. Ross had died intestate.

---

[167] *Queensland, Australia, Immigration Indexes, 1848-1972.*, viewed 24-04-2024 https://www.ancestry.com.au/

[168] *Australia, Death Index 1787-1985*, viewed 24-04-2024 https://www.ancestry.com.au/

Alexander, her younger brother, had been appointed administrator of Ross's estate. Tom Cook took Alexander Ross to court and was subsequently awarded the Balnagowan property in 1914. It was determined that the Cooks were to have the Balnagowan property and the Ross family the Calrossie property, also located near Mackay.[169]

Joining her husband at Balnagowan, near Mackay sometime after 1865, Cook had the misfortune to lose her daughter, Alexandria, at the age of 4. She was helping her mother wash clothes on the bank of the river when her dress caught alight from an open fire. Medical assistance came from 12 miles away, but she died of her injuries.[170] Life must have been difficult in those days (1867), when living in remote areas without modern conveniences to aid in household tasks and medical assistance was not as advanced or readily available as today.

Five further children were born to Elizabeth and John Cook: John Thomas Robert,[171] born 2 December 1868 and died at Scone in 1896; Cecilia Adelaide Maud Cook Thompson, born 31 January 1871 and died 7 January 1951; Charles Edmund, born 3 May 1873 and died 8 May 1873; Albert Alfred Cook born 4 September 1875 and died 24 March 1948; and Ethel Victoria Octavia Cook Glenny, born 14 April 1878 and died in 1962.[172]

A special weatherboard building was erected at Balnagowan as a schoolhouse. Mackay district did not have a government school until 1871.[173] Cook was the children's teacher in the 'school room'

---

[169] Clark, Betty, 1992, *A House Well Filled*, Mackay, Mackay Printing & Publishing, pp. 22-23.
[170] Gcasandra, 2018, '10 Pioneering Women Who Shaped Mackay's Future', viewed 12/04/2024 https://www.couriermail.com.au/queensland/mackay/
[171] John Robert Cook became a Doctor of Medicine and died 'by his own hand' at the age of 28 years. An inquest was held, and the jury gave a verdict of suicide while temporarily insane. 'Suicide at Scone, 1896, *Maitland Weekly Mercury*, 25 April p.14., viewed 12/04/2024 http://nla.gov.au/nla.news-article132403608.
[172] *Death in the District of Mackay in the State of Queensland*, 1907, 'Elizabeth Cormack Ross Cook', Mackay, The Government.
[173] Hall, Glen, 2022, *Mackay School History*, viewed 16/04/2024, https://www.mackayhistory.org/research/schools/schools.html

at Balnagowan until they reached secondary school level when they were sent to private colleges in NSW. Albert and his younger sister Ethel attended George Perkins Private School which specialised in individual instruction for various business examinations and guided them for entrance to private schools in the south. Albert was sent to New England Grammar School in Armidale while his sister Ethel attended the Presbyterian Ladies School at Armidale.[174]

Elizabeth Cook died in 1907 at the age of 72. She had lived the life of an early settler coming to terms with the death of three of her children and the hardships of living in an unfamiliar and unknown tropical environment. She was buried in Walkerston Cemetery near Mackay.

Events:

- 1860 Arrived in New South Wales
- 1865 Arrived at Balnagowan near Mackay
- 1914 Formal ownership of Balnagowan estate

Figure 16 The School at Balnagowan. Photograph courtesy of *The Courier Mail.*

---

[174] Bowden, Vicky, 2021, 'Home education is an Old Concept with New Challenges, *Daily Mercury*, 17 February, viewed 7/05/2024 http://www.dailymercury.com.au

Cook, Vida Althaea (1875-1955)

Figure 17 Vida Althaea Cook. Photograph courtesy of the Greenmount Historic Homestead Collection.

Born:
- 6 April 1875
- 'Woonon', near Sarina, south of Mackay, Queensland

Died:
- 27 September 1955
- Mackay, Queensland

Occupation:
- Artist, nurse, diarist, grazier and philanthropist. Atherton's marriage into the Cook family cemented two grazing dynasties into one.

Alternative Name/s
- Vida Cook, Althaea Cook, Vida Atherton, Althaea Atherton.

Summary:

Vida was the third daughter of Richard Atherton and Letitia Janet Orr Atherton, and one of eight children, four girls and four boys, the youngest two being twins. The Athertons were originally from Lancashire in England, the descendants of farmers for many generations. Edmund and Esther Atherton with their family sailed from England aboard the *Briton* and arrived in Sydney on 28 June 1844.[175] They settled in the Armidale area of NSW, later establishing properties in the Rockhampton district in Queensland (which at that time was a part of NSW) and as far north as the Atherton Tablelands. A diary was kept by Richard Atherton, a hobby taken up by his daughter, Vida.[176]

Atherton started writing a diary in 1887 at the age of 12 when the family had moved to Howard Park Station a few miles south of Mackay. Excursion from their property into Mackay involved riding a horse or taking the buggy to shop for gifts. In her diary, she describes the gas lights that lit the town at night. Other excursions were to attend christenings, having dinners with friends or attending the circus in much the same way as we do today. On another occasion they rode into Mackay and stayed with friends for a week and enjoyed activities while in town. One longer trip was to Rockhampton, horse-back riding by day and camping by night. The trip took ten days one way. They stayed a week and then returned home.[177]

Atherton's artistic abilities blossomed from the time she was about 17 years old. Her many pencil sketches and water colour paintings are in various collections, namely at Greenmount Homestead, and diary records held at James Cook University in Townsville. One of her sketches was of highland sheep and guardian dogs signed

---

[175] New South Wales, Australia, 1844, *Assisted Immigrant Passenger Lists, 1828-1896*, viewed 19/04/2024 https://www.ancestry.com.au/
[176] Clark, Betty, 1992, *A House Well Filled*, Mackay, Historical Society and Museum, pp. 51-60.
[177] ibid., pp.57-59.

and dated in 1892 at the age of 17. A small notebook records the comment, 'I finished the sheep drawing today, 13 May 1892.' [178]

Leaving the family in Mackay, her father's diary entries indicated that Atherton worked as a nurse at the Children's Hospital in Brisbane. Over a two-year period, she found the tasks of nursing sick children under the supervision of an 'ill-tempered' matron somewhat arduous, and she missed the family, so she decided to return to Mackay. In 1903, she began to spend more time at Balnagowan.[179] Therefore, it was not surprising when her engagement to Albert Alfred Cook was announced. They were engaged for a period of twelve months. Albert (as he was known) was the second youngest child and youngest son of Elizabeth Cormack Ross and John Cook of Balnagowan near Mackay.

The marriage took place in the drawing-room of the Atherton home of the bride at Howard Park, tastefully decorated with flowers, ferns and pot plants. The ceremony had been delayed due to wet weather and took place on Saturday afternoon on 11 April 1908. The bride wore an ivory white silk dress with a tulle veil from Belfast, Ireland and her hair was adorned by orange blossoms. Her sister Ina and the groom's sister Ethel Cook were bridesmaids. The bride's sister Emily played the piano, an example of the cultural education given to young ladies of those times who had limited opportunities to enter the workforce as domestics, nurses, or governesses. The wedding ceremony was extensively covered by local newspapers.[180]

The newlyweds took an extended honeymoon of about three months, visiting Turanville (the Cook family property) and Scone, Brisbane and Sydney, including Bundaberg and Rockhampton by train and steamer from Rockhampton to Mackay on their return journey. They took a tender from the Pioneer River wharf

---

[178] Clark, Betty, op. cit., p.64.
[179] ibid., pp.59-60.
[180] 'Wedding Bells: Cook Atherton', 1908, *Daily Mercury*, 13 April, p.3., viewed 20/01/2024 http://nla.gov.au/nla.news.-article170789685

transferring to a steamer the *SS Bombala* anchored off flat top island. This was no ordinary boat, providing three-course gourmet meals. Their visit to Sydney took in the major tourist attractions by tram, the theatre, zoo and museum and the many beach suburbs of Manly and Watson's Bay. Several items of furniture such as the 'chiffonier' were purchased whilst in Sydney.[181] Cook continued to paint water colours during her honeymoon, all signed 'V.A. Cook'. Most of her artwork is stored at Greenmount Historic Homestead.

The family grew with the birth of Thomas Albert (Tom) Cook on 14 January 1910 at Dr Williams private hospital, the Ormond Hospital, Mackay. Cook and son were driven home in a new 'motor buggy' by husband Albert. The birth of John Alfred Cook followed (1912-1929) and daughter Althea Atherton Cook Kelsey Parsons (1915-1976). Unfortunately for the family, John Alfred suffered with diabetes for four years and died at the age of 17.[182]

Albert Cook purchased Greenmount Station in 1913 from the Pleystowe Mill Land Syndicate.[183] This land was formerly owned by Mackay's founder, John Mackay, who took up the land in 1862. The Greenmount Homestead was designed by architect William Sykes. A garden surrounds the house. The family moved into the house in 1915. The homestead and surrounding property are now a museum managed by the local council.

Cook was witness to some of the advances in technology and landmark events that impacted the Mackay district. The 1920s and 30s were an exciting time for the Cooks living in Mackay. They founded the first Aberdeen Angus stud in North Queensland by purchasing some Black Poll bulls and heifers from New Zealand. A tennis court was built in 1929 at Greenmount which became an attraction in the 1940s when American servicemen were entertained by the Cooks.

---

[181] Clark, Betty, 1992, op. cit., pp. 64-65.
[182] *Death in the District of Mackay in the State of Queensland*, 1955, 'Vida Althea Cook', Mackay, The Government.
[183] ibid., p.73.

The first aircraft landed at Ooralea on the racecourse in September of 1920. The first radio broadcast occurred in Sydney in 1923. Electricity was installed in Mackay in 1924. The Cooks purchased land at what was then called Seaview but now called Bucasia to build a holiday house. Sir Charles Kingsford Smith offered joy flights around the Mackay district which Tom Cook took advantage of and flew with 'Smithy'. Holiday options broadened in the district when Eungella Chalet was opened by Premier Scullin in 1934, and trips to Brampton Island were possible aboard the *SS Woy Woy*. Travelling further afield for holidays Cook and daughter, Althea sailed to Townsville via Flat Top Island and took a train to visit Atherton relatives in Townsville and the Atherton Tableland which was named after Vida's family.

Althea Cook was briefly married and divorced between 1939 and 1946 to Ralph Kelsey. She later remarried. During World War II, Greenmount Homestead became a centre for entertainment of American servicemen holding tennis matches, and weekend stays with daughter Althea becoming a Red Cross Volunteer. Personal links were established between the Cooks and Eleanore Roosvelt, first lady of the United States of America. Cook received a letter from the American Red Cross Service Club of Mackay, sending her Christmas greetings in December of 1943.[184] She was also an active member of Presbyterian Church and supported the Country Women's Association (CWA).

With the marriage of Tom and Dorothy Cook, Cook and her daughter Althea retired to their holiday home at Bucasia. Vida and Albert's financial interests were broad. She held shares in the Pleystowe Land Syndicate as did Albert, as well as being involved with Albert in the financial and business dealings of Pleystowe Mill. They were involved in many businesses and philanthropic activities throughout the district. Vida Cook died in 1955, aged

---

[184] Fisher, Dora, 1943, *American Red Cross Service Club*, 16 Pirie Street, Mackay, 23 December. James Cook University, Special Collections, Vida Cook Collection, Townsville, Queensland.

80 years, five years after her son Tom's marriage to Dorothy Drysdale. Both Cook and her husband were buried in Walkerston Cemetery near Mackay.

Events:

- 1887 Began keeping a dairy of events
- 1892 Began to compile works of art
- 1900 Began two years of nursing
- 1908 Married Albert Alfred Cook
- 1915 Moved from Balnagowan to Greenmount Homestead
- 1930s Founded the Aberdeen Angus Stud at Greenmount
- 1940s Provided entertainment for US Servicemen

Links:

Design & Art Australia Online https://www.daao.org.au/bio/version_history/vida-althea-atherton/recognitions/?p=2&revision_no=3

Figure 18 Vida Atherton as a nurse circa 1902. Photograph courtesy the Greenmount Historic Homestead collection.

Cooke, Jane (1812-1888)

Figure 19 Royal Hotel at the corner Sydney & Victoria Streets, Mackay 1871. Photograph courtesy of Mackay Historical Society.

Born:
- 3 October 1812
- Marylebone, London, England, United Kingdom

Died:
- 28 May 1888
- Allenstown, Rockhampton, Queensland

Occupation:
- Hotel Licensee for the Royal Hotel, Sydney Street, Mackay. Once a convict, Cooke created a new life for herself in the colonies by becoming hostess of events attended by the Governor of Queensland.

Alternative names/s:
- Jane Harris, Jane Cook.

Summary:

Jane Harris was the only daughter of Job Harris and Sarah Hopkins who were married in St James Westminster, London, England on 17 March 1803. Jane was baptised on 27 October 1812 at Saint Mary-St, Marylebone Road, St Marylebone London England. At the age of 21, on 18 July in 1833, she was convicted of stealing stockings and cheese from her employer at the Compton Abbas Assize,[185] a village and civil parish in North Dorset. Harris may also have had an accomplice to her crime as the court record indicates that Samuel Down was charged with the same crime, on the same day by the same accuser, John Hussey Esquire. Samuel Down was acquitted on 20 July 1833.[186] Harris's attitude and behaviour while incarcerated was recorded as one of insolence and she was charged with assaulting and beating a 17-year-old female inmate (Hannah Viccars) for which she received a sentence of four days in her cell.[187]

Her initial sentence for stealing was seven years transportation to Van Diemen's Land (Hobart Town, Tasmania). She sailed from Woolwich, London, on 5 May 1834 aboard the sailing ship, *Edward*, arriving in Hobart Town on 4 September of that year, one of 151 female convicts.[188]

Harris married Francis Goude Cooke, nine years her senior, on 5 December 1836 in Hobart Town. Francis was born at Stoke Damerel, Plymouth, England on 12 May 1836, to William Cooke and Margaret Goude. Harris was 24 years old at the time of her marriage, just two years after arriving in Hobart, and five years prior to the end of her sentence. As a convict, Harris would have sought permission to marry.[189]

---

[185] An Assize was a court which formerly sat at intervals in each county of England and Wales to administer the civil and criminal law. In 1972 the civil jurisdiction of assizes was transferred to the High Court, and the criminal jurisdiction to the Crown Court.

[186] Ancestry.com.au, 2023, *Jane Harris in the Dorset England Dorchester Prison Admission and Discharge Registers, 1782-1901*, viewed 15/12/2023 https://www.ancestry.com.au

[187] State library and Archives Services, Tasmania, 2023, emailed information, librariestasmania@researchservices.info 19 December, 2023.

[188] Uebel, Lesley, 1998, *Claim a Convict: Details for the Ship Edward 1834*, viewed 22/12/2023 https://www.hawkesbury.net.au/claimaconvict/shipDetails.php?ship...

[189] State Library and Archive Service, Tasmania, 2023, email from librariestasmania@researchservices.info received December 19.

The Cookes had nine children born in Tasmania: Jemima (Mima) Marjory (born 7 November 1837 and died 1878); Mary Ann (born 23 July 1839 and died 1916); Emma Ellen (born 1841 and died 1901); Jane Eliza (born 23 August 1843 and did 1864); Frances Goude (born 2 October 1845 and died 1912); Francis Goude (born August 1848 and died 1855); Clara Kate (born 28 July 1849 and died 1859); William Daniel (born 21 December 1851 and died 15 Apil 1908); and Corinna (born 15 February 1854 and died 1920). Jane's husband Francis Cooke died in Launceston on 19 February 1859. He had been the publican of the Masons Arms Hotel in Launceston.[190]

Following the death of her husband and daughter Clara in 1859, Jane and her remaining children travelled north to Mackay. Having experience with hotel life in Launceston, Cooke leased the Royal Hotel on the corner of Sydney and Victoria Streets in 1865. She applied for a publican's licence to sell fermented and spiritous liquors, promoting herself as a widow with five children and advertising her hotel as having five sitting rooms and ten bedrooms. She had to have been made of 'stern stuff' as indicated by her earlier life experiences, to withstand the rough-and-tumble of a publican's life in a colonial town in north Queensland.[191]

Hotel life meant hosting many local events such as local council meetings, political meetings, meetings of planters, the Turf Club and Show Society, as well as the Cattle Stealing Prevention Association. At a farewell dinner for a local bank manager, it was reported that ... 'a sumptuous repast was served up in Mrs Cooke's best style and good taste.'[192] A reception and banquet was held at the Royal when the Governor of Queensland, Lord Russell Phipps, visited Mackay in 1872 and 1874.[193]

---

[190] Mackay Family History Society, 2012, 'Jane Cooke Hotelier 1865', Mackay, The Society.
[191] ibid.
[192] ibid.
[193] ibid.

Korah Wills came to Mackay from Townsville in 1870 and purchased the land and premises of Cooke's Royal Hotel and renamed it the Wills Hotel. Cooke then built a one-storey brick hotel in Sydney Street nearer North Street (now River Street) and named it the Royal Hotel. It was near to John Allen's store and not far from the Pioneer River. In 1972, it doubled in size by the addition of a second building. Cooke held the license for this hotel until 1880.

Cooke died of 'senile decay' at West Street, Allenstown, Rockhampton on 28 May 1888, aged 75. She was buried at Rockhampton Cemetery. She overcame many obstacles, managed a large family and achieved a social status that she may not have been open to her if she had not been transported to Australia.

Events:

- 1833 Sentenced to seven years transportation to Van Diemen's Land
- 1834 Arrived in Australia
- 1865-1870 Held a publican's licence in Mackay, Queensland

Cronin, Amelia (1894-1972)

Figure 20 Amelia Morley Box Cronin
Photograph courtesy of Ancestry.com

Born:
- 17 August 1894
- 8 Walton Row, Leeds, Yorkshire West Riding, England

Died:
- 21 March 1972
- Mater Hospital, Mackay

Occupation:
- Hotel Licensee for the Grand Central Hotel, Sarina, Gargett Hotel, Railway Hotel in Marian, and Mirani Hotel. Cronin overcame significant disadvantage early in life to become one of the well-known and respected publicans in the Mackay district.

Alternative names/s:
- Amelia Morely, Amelia Box, Amelia Styran/m

Summary:

Amelia Morley was born to Annie Morley, a tailoress, and father unknown, at 8 Walton Row, Leeds, Yorkshire West Riding. Her baptism certificate does not record a father's name. She was baptised on 5 September 1894 at St Barnabas Church, Holbeck, County of York.[194] Little is known about her early life in England except that her mother died in an infirmary when Amelia was 16 months old. She was in an orphanage and then fostered out to a family by the name of Walter and Fanny Perry Styran and given the first name of Emily. A second baptism for Amelia Morley took place in the name of Emily Styran in 1900 although there is no birth record for a female child of this name. It is believed that this was Amelia Morley.[195]

Following the death of her foster mother Fanny, her stepfather married Alice Abson in 1903. The family (Walter, Alice and three children, one of whom was Alice's daughter from a previous relationship) travelled aboard the vessel *'Gothic'* to New Zealand in 1905 and returned to London in April 1906 aboard the vessel *Ionic*. The family, with Amelia (as Emily), then at the age of 16, arrived in Brisbane in 1909 aboard the vessel *Perthshire*.[196]

The marriage between Morley and Walter Charles Box on 3 April 1912 at the Baptist Manse in Maryborough, resulted in duplicate marriage entries in Ancestry. One entry was for the marriage of Amelia Styram and the other as Amelia Morely. She was 18 years old. The family had two daughters, Amelia Clarice born 11 February 1914 at Gladstone, and another deceased female child.[197] The surname Styram was associated with Amelia's surname on her daughter, Amelia Clarice Box's family tree.

---

[194] Queensland State Library, 2023, 'Amelia Morley', Brisbane, The Library, slqaskus@libraryresearch.info
[195] Mackay Family History Society, 2012, 'Amelia Cronin', Mackay, The Society.
[196] ibid.
[197] *Queensland Government, Births, Deaths, Marriages*, 1972, 'Death: Amelia Cronin', Mackay, The Government, viewed 25/09/2023 https://www.qld.gov.au/law/births-deaths-marriages-and-divorces/family-history-research

The family lived in Ferry Lane, Maryborough prior to moving to Mackay. Her husband worked as a labourer in 1919. 'For a time, Amelia had a convenience store on the corner of Carlyle and Victoria Streets (now the Buffalo Club). Local fishermen from the River Streets wharves were very good customers and obtained all their supplies from the store. Box eventually rented the store to her daughter.'[198]

The couple were reported to be on good terms until 1924 when Box obtained the license for the Grand Central hotel, Sarina. This was granted on 7 January 1925. On 16 September 1925, Box became the licensee of the Coronation Hotel in Gargett. She was publican there for three years during which time she divorced Walter Box.[199] The relationship took a downward turn during that time. The experience of working in a hotel seemed detrimental to her husband's health.

The hotel was sold in August of 1925 after Walter Box was hospitalised following a suicide attempt. Upon his release from hospital, he refused to live with his wife. In November of that year, Box engaged a private detective and went to a 'humpy' in Maryborough, where she and the Detective found her husband by torch light. They observed that was engaged in an extra-marital affair with a woman named in a petition for a decree nisi (divorce), which was granted by the Judge in November of 1927.[200] Cronin was about 31 years of age.

Marriage laws in the colonies closely followed those of the *English Marriage Act* of 1936. 'Prior to 1961, the states had their own statutes of divorce, all of which had their origin in the *English Divorce Act* of 1857.'[201] Proof of matrimonial fault was

---
[198] Mackay Family History Society, 2012, op. cit.
[199] Peberdy, Yvonne, 2024, email confirmed on Wednesday 22 May 2024.
[200] 'Divorce Granted', 1927, *Daily Standard*, Thursday 14 1927, p.4., viewed 28/09/2023, http://nla.gov.au/nla.news-article179466725
[201] Krishnamoorthy, Sowrirajulu, 1987, 'Changing Marriage and Divorce Patterns in Australia: 1921-81: An Application of Multi-State Life Table Analysis', *Luglio-Dicembre*, vol. 43, no.3/4 pp.69-84.

usually required for a divorce to take place. Inconsistencies in divorce legislation between the states led the Federal Parliament to enact the *Matrimonial Causes Act* of 1959. The Act came into effect in 1961 standardising the grounds for divorce throughout Australia, although the grounds for divorce still required fault to be apportioned. A separation period of five years was also required.[202] Therefore, Box was required to apportion fault in her marriage to enable a divorce to take place in the 1920s.

Box then became licensee of the Coronation Hotel in Gargett from 1925 until 1928. She divorced Walter Box in 1927 and on May 30, 1928, and married Francis (Frank) Melody Cronin (1897-1973) in Mackay.[203] The couple went on to have two children; Eileen Frances Cronin Goan (1929-1993) and Brian Cronin (1934-2018).[204]

In 1928, Cronin became the licensee and the owner of the Railway Hotel, Marian, purchasing it in 1932. During the Second World War, the Railway Hotel was a popular venue for United States servicemen on leave in Mackay. Taxi drivers were known to transport servicemen from Mackay to the railway Hotel, a distance of approximately 28 km to purchase alcohol. Whisky was about two shillings and sixpence a bottle. Amelia and Frank sold the Marian Hotel on 7 November 1947 for the sum of £5,000 to Claude Ernest Smith of Rockhampton.[205] The transfer went through in 1948, and Amelia joined Frank in the Mirani Hotel.

The Cronins held the license for the Mirani Hotel in 1942. They extended that lease for another seven years and in 1952 they purchased it freehold from Louisa Feltham for £16,000. Ownership of the hotel continued in the family until 2017 when

---

[202] ibid.
[203] Hall, Glenn, 2017, *Publicans and Licensees of Mackay*, viewed 26/09/2023, http://mackayhistory.org/research/publicans/
[204] *Death in the District of Mackay in the State of Queensland*, 1972, 'Amelia Cronin', Mackay, The Government.
[205] Mackay Family History Society, 2012, op. cit.

it was sold. Cronin died at the age of 77 and was buried on 22 March 1972 at Mt Bassett Cemetery. DNA research undertaken by her grandson Scott has revealed that Walter, her adopted father was in fact her biological father.[206] Her husband Frank died the following year.

Events:

- 1909 Arrived in Brisbane
- 1924 – 1925 Grand Central Hotel, Sarina
- 1928 Coronation Hotel Gargett
- 1928 – 1947 Railway Hotel, Marian Hotel
- 1942 - 1972 Mirani Hotel, Mirani

Figure 21 Mirani Hotel 2017. Photograph courtesy of *The Courier Mail.*

---

[206] Peberdy, Yvonne, op. cit.

Derrer, Sister Mary Jane (1892-1986) MM

**Figure 22 Sister Mary Jane Derrer.
Photograph courtesy of the Virtual War Memorial Australia.**

Born:
- 3 February 1892
- Homebush, Mackay, Queensland, Australia

Died:
- 19 January 1986
- Nudgee Cemetery, Nudgee, Brisbane City, Queensland, Australia

Occupation:
- Staff nurse, sister, servicewoman in World War I, Anzac. Derrer was one of a few Australian nurses during the First World War to be awarded the Military Medal.

Alternative name/s:
- Mary Gallagher

Summary:

Mary Jane Derrer was the youngest surviving child of Josepha (Wannmeister) and Gottfried Derrer, farmers at Homebush and Chelona.[207] Both Josepha and Gottfried emigrated from Switzerland. They married in Queensland in July of 1873.[208]

Derrer trained as a nurse at the Mackay Base Hospital from March 1910 to March 1911[209] and was a member of the Australasian Trained Nurses Association (ATNA) (1899) Australia's first nursing association.[210] She also worked at the Lister Hospital in Mackay prior to enlisting in the Australian Imperial Force (AIF), unit No 2 Australian General Hospital, on 12 July 1915 at the age of 24 years. She was a staff nurse with the Australian Army Nursing Service (AANS).[211] Her service record describes her as being 5'8" tall, weighing 140 lbs, having black hair, brown eyes and a dark complexion. Her religion was listed as Roman Catholic. She passed through the Military Hospital at Kangaroo Point. One of her older sisters, Rosine Derrer - (born 5 October 1885), also enlisted as a trained nurse, thirteen months later in August of 1916. Another sister, Anna Waters of Homebush, was nominated as Mary Jane and Rosine's next of kin.

---

[207] Australian Electoral Commission, 1913, *Australia, Electoral Rolls, 1903-1980*, Canberra, The Commonwealth, viewed 2023-01-11 https://mail.google.com/mail/
[208] Ancestry.com, 2023, *Australia, Marriage Index, 1788-1950*, viewed 2023-01-05, http://ancestry.com.au.
[209] 'Personal Notes', 1917, *Brisbane Courier*, Tuesday 2 October, p. 7, viewed 2023-01-05 http://nla.gov.au/nla-news-article20190454
[210] *The Australian Women's Register*, 2023, viewed 2023-01-11 https://www.womenaustralia.info/biogs/AWE0973b.htm
The Australasian Trained Nurses' Association (ATNA), Australia's first nursing association, was formed in New South Wales in 1899, with branches subsequently established in Queensland in 1904, South Australia in 1905, Western Australia in 1907 and Tasmania in 1908. It sought to improve the status of nurses through registration and to develop standards of training in hospital schools of nursing. The Association commenced publication of its journal entitled *Australasian Nurses' Journal*, (ANJ) in 1904. The state branches eventually came to form branches of the Australian Nursing Federation, which was established in 1924.
[211] NAA: B2455 Derrer, MJ, 1915, Canberra, *National Archives Australia*, viewed 2023-12-22 https://recordsearch.naa.gov.au

Derrer embarked for Egypt with reinforcements for the 2nd Casualty Clearing Station (2nd CCS), from Sydney on 14 July 1915 aboard *HMAT Orsova A67*. On arrival in Egypt, she joined the 2nd CCS, then treating Australian soldiers wounded at Gallipoli. In 1916, with the AIF moving to the Western Front in France, the 2nd CCS deployed to Trois Arbres, France.[212]

Late in the evening of the 22 July 1917 the hospital at the 2nd ACCS, in Trois Arbes, was bombed by enemy aircraft. In an act of great bravery, Sisters Mary Jane Derrer, Clare Deacon, Dorothy Cawood and Alice Ross-King heroically rescued patients trapped in burning hospital tents. 'Witness accounts describe nurses running to tents shattered by bombs to rescue patients, either carrying them to safety or placing tables over patient's beds to protect them. All four women were subsequently awarded the Military Medal for their heroism.'[213] 'It was the first time the British award for 'bravery and devotion under fire', had been bestowed on nurses in any theatre of war.'[214] The Military Medal was awarded on 25 September 1917. Also in 1917, Mary Jane was attached to Harefield House Hospital in England (No.1 Australian Auxiliary Hospital), which was used as a hospital for soldiers from December 1914 to January 1919.[215]

It was also during 1917 that Derrer was discharged from the AIF for medical reasons - she had a spinal injury. Her medical records do not indicate the cause of the injury, although nursing was physically stressful, especially during a war and without any automated aids to assist. Nurses lacked medical supplies, fresh

---

[212] Gallagher, Bob, 2023, 'Mary Jane (Derrer) Gallagher MM (1892-1986)', *Wiktree*, viewed 2023-01-04 https://www.wikitree/Derrer-69#Biography

[213] *Commonwealth of Australia Gazette*, 1918, 'Sister Mary Jane Derrer', Thursday 24 January, p.79., *Australian War Memorial*, viewed 20/02/2024, https://www.awm.gov.au/collection/P11051273

[214] Women of the North, 2018, *Mary Jane Derrer MM, viewed 2023-01-03* https://womenofthenorth.blog/2018/11/11/mary-jane-derrer/m-m

[215] 'Harefield House Hospital No.1 Australian Auxiliary Hospital', 2023, *Australian War Memorial*, viewed 2023-01-13 https://www.awm.gov.au/articles/encyclopedia/harefield

water and faced the difficulty of keeping wounds and patients clean. She re-enlisted in March of 1918 and subsequently saw service in India. Following her return to Australia in 1919, she nursed at the Kangaroo Point Military Hospital and then continued her nursing career in Mackay at the Lister Private Hospital.

Derrer was reluctant to write about her experiences and only gave a description of the routine and practical aspects of war nursing in Flanders, which portrayed a steadfast adherence to duty at a time when a continuous stream of casualties was arriving from the trenches. Some casualties stayed for many weeks; others passed on. A comment in the *Queenslander* in 1918 depicts the fierce fighting during the Battle of Messines in 1917 as putting a great strain on the capacity of the hospital and its workers; thousands of cases had to handled, both friends and foe as well as civilian casualties.[216]

Rosine, Mary's sister, (1885-1925), wrote an account of her experiences during the First World War which is held by the Australian War Memorial. Staff nurse Rosine's service record indicates she was gravely ill with jaundice while serving in India in 1918 and survived. Derrer joined the AIF at 29 years of age (in 1916) as a staff nurse and was promoted to the rank of Sister prior to returning to Australia on 8 August 1919. She was awarded the 1914-1915 Star, British War Medal and Victory Medal.[217] Sister Rosine married James Arthur Bennett on 3 June 1925 in Brisbane. She died in Brisbane on 4 May 1975.

Mary Jane Derrer married Dr Michael Joseph (Joe) Gallagher with whom she had three children. These were, Madeleine Mary, Maurice John and Andrew Godfrey Patrick. Dr Joe Gallagher had married previously, and his wife died in childbirth. Gallagher and her husband attended Anzac Day services both in Mackay

---

[216] Women's Department: A Nurses Experience', 2018, *Queenslander*, Saturday 2 February, p.5.
[217] NAA B2455, Derrer R., 1915, Canberra, *National Archives of Australia*, viewed 2022-12-23 Https://recordseacrh.naa.gov.au

and in Sydney. She moved to Brisbane in later years and died on 19 January 1986 at the Lillian Cooper Nursing Home, Kangaroo Point aged 93 years.[218]

In 1917, five Australian nurses were awarded the Military Medal. Sister Mary Jane Derrer of Mackay, Queensland was one of them.[219] In 1918 there was only one Military Medal awarded in Australia. These brave women and the many others who lost their lives or who were injured in the service of others, deserve to be remembered.

Events:

- World War 1 Service:
  - 12 Jul 1915: **Enlisted** Australian Army Nursing Service (WW1) Staff Nurse, Brisbane, Queensland
  - 14 Jul 1915: **Involvement** Australian Army Nursing Service (WW1), Staff Nurse, 2nd Australian General Hospital, AIF
  - Enlistment/Embarkation WW1
  - 14 Jul 1915: **Embarked** Australian Army Nursing Service (WW1), Staff Nurse, SN Nurse, 2nd Australian General Hospital, AIF
  - HMAT Orsova, Sydney
  - 25 Sep 1917: **Awarded** the Military Medal
  - 28 Dec 1917: **Discharged** Australian Army Nursing Service (WW1), Staff Nurse, 1st Australian General Hospital
  - 25 Mar 1918: **Enlisted** Australian Army Nursing Service (WW1), Staff Nurse
  - 25 Sep 1918: **Promoted** Australian Army Nursing Service (WW1), Sister

---

[218] *Deaths in the District of Brisbane in the State of Queensland*, 1975, 'Mary Jane Gallagher', Brisbane, The Government.
[219] 'Faith, Hope, Charity Australian Women and Imperial Honours: 1901-1989', viewed 2023-01-03 https://www.womenaustralia.info/exhib/honours/mm.html

- 9 Nov 1918: **Embarked** Australian Army Nursing Service (WW1) Sister, Australian Army Nursing Service (WW1), HMAT Wiltshire, Sydney
- 9 Nov 1918: **Involvement** Australian Army Nursing Service (WW1), Sister
- Enlistment/Embarkation WW1
- 27 Jan 1920: **Discharged** Australian Army Nursing Service (WW1), Sister[220]

Awards:

- 1914-1915 Star
- British War Medal
- Victory Medal
- Military Medal

Links:

Australian War Memorial https://www.awm.gov.au/collection/P11051273

Virtual War Memorial Australia https://vwma.org.au/explore/people/207850

---

[220] NAA: B2455, Derrer M J, 1915, *National Archives of Australia*, op. cit.

Finger, Hilda (1891-1916)

Figure 23 Hilda Finger aged 17 years.
Photograph courtesy of Mackay Family History Society.

Born:
- 23 April 1891
- Mackay, Queensland

Died:
- 22 November 1916
- Peel Island, Moreton Bay, Queensland

Occupation:
- Tailoress and maid. Finger had a brief life, suffering with leprosy from a young age and dying at the age of 25.

Summary:

There was nothing remarkable in the childhood of young Hilda who was the fifth child of Hermann Julius Finger and Marie Wilhelmine Auguste Wendtland, to indicate that she would have a tragic life. Hermann Finger had three brothers and six sisters. He was 6 years old when his parents immigrated to Australia arriving in 1886 aboard the *Wandrahm*, which was quarantined at Dunwich for about three months. Hilda's mother, Auguste Wendtland, was born in Germany in 1862 and migrated with her parents when she was 21, arriving aboard the *Duke of Buckingham* in 1883, settling near Beenleigh with the German community at Bethania. As the German communities in Queensland were in close communication that was possibly how the couple met.[221] The family were sent by the Government to Bowen to assist with the building of the town's jetty. They later moved to Mackay. In Mackay, the family owned a house on five acres of land in George Street.

The children were William Herman Francis Finger (1885-1967); Elizabeth Henriette Finger Flor (1885-1967); Henrietta Louisa Finger Vollbon (1888-1973); Ellen Hermine Finger Andersen (1889-1973); Hermina Finger Willman Brown (1893-1984); Louise Marie Finger Pershouse (1894-1980); Ida Auguste Finger Kogler (1895-?); Herman Otto Finger (1900-1972); and Walter Gustav Finger (1906-1980).[222]

Finger was first employed as a maid then as a tailoress. She was admitted to the Mackay Base Hospital on 29 July 1907 at the age of 16. It is unclear from the hospital entry what she was suffering from or when she was discharged.[223] Doctor Stewart Kay was reported to have diagnosed her with bacillus leprae (leprosy or Hansen's disease) in October of 1910. Within seven days of this diagnosis, the Government Home Secretary ordered her to be removed and detained at the Lazarette (leprosarium) on

---

[221] Ludlow, Peter, 2000, *Moreton Bay People: The Complete Collection*, Stones Corner, Queensland, Peter Ludlow.
[222] *Deaths in the District of Bundaberg in the State of Queensland, Agusta Maria Wilhelmina Finger*, 1941, Bundaberg, The Government.
[223] Queensland Government, 1907, *Mackay Hospital Admissions 1891 to 1908: Hilda Finger*, 29 July, viewed 6/12/2023 https://www.archivessearch.qld.gov.au/items/ITM1001210

Peel Island in Moreton Bay.[224] Finger was cared for by her sister Louisa on a farm located near where the Mackay airport is today, until transport was arranged to Peel Island. Louisa would walk into town and purchase groceries, keeping the receipts which were refunded by the government. The farmer, Robert Cutting, increased the rent on the house possibly due to builders refusing to work on a new house near where Finger was living.[225]

Transport to and from Mackay was by sea in the early 1900s. There was no rail or road link between Mackay and Brisbane. It was five months before the hastily constructed wooden crate could be built for the steamer *Porpoise*, that had an all-male crew and they slept below, hence the need for a 'crate'. Hilda was rowed out to the steamer that left from Flat Top Island on 20 March 1911. The crate which sat on the deck was to be her home for the journey to Moreton Bay without any luggage or facilitates for her own care. On arrival at Peel Island, a similar process of rowing the crate with Hilda inside to the beach was undertaken. The crate was subsequently burnt on the beach. She was met by the superintendent of the Lazaret. A horse and dray transported her to the other end of the Island where the huts were located.[226]

Finger's home on Peel Island consisted of a 10ft by 12ft hut containing a bed, chair, table and chest of drawers. Visitors were few and infrequent. Once installed in her accommodation, a medical examination was undertaken on 27 March 1911.[227] A written report indicated some aspects of the state of her heath were as follows: that several years prior, a sore under the ball of the left big toe was troublesome to heal; the fingers on both hands were slightly swollen; the skin on her chest, back of neck and shoulders was scaly and discoloured; and the disease had advanced steadily since admission. Although the disease was far

---

[224] Mackay Family History Society, 2012, 'Hilda Finger: Tailoress 1891', Mackay, The Society.
[225] Flor, Noel, 2024, *Interview*, 3 June.
[226] Ludlow, Peter, 1996, *Peel Island: Paradise or Prison*, Stones Corner, Qld, p.159.
[227] ibid.

advanced, the Doctor (unnamed in the report) thought that there was a chance of considerably improving the girl's condition if she could be persuaded to persevere with a proper line of treatment.[228]

One of the early treatment methods was to isolate the patient. Little was understood about the disease in the early 1900s. It was not until 1944 during the Second World War that penicillin was used to treat soldiers serving in Papua New Guinea. Leprosy is now considered a rare disease in Australia. If detected it can be easily treated and cured by antibiotics.

The lack of knowledge and fear surrounding the disease in the early 1900s was immense. The impact on her family was overwhelming. Her parents were overcome with grief and never really came to terms with the tragedy that changed their lives forever. Her father Hermann was unable to sell the George Street house, so he burned the house to the ground. He later sold the five acres of land on which the house was located. He also lost his job at Cameron's Foundry where he had worked for over twenty years. His co-workers refused to work with him for fear of catching the disease. Her two sisters, Ellen and Hermine who were employed as a Milliner with Sharp and Dellar were dismissed when Finger's disease became public. Fear and ignorance of catching leprosy was like the reaction of the more recent global pandemic of HIV/AIDS which began in 1981.[229]

Finger died from cardiac failure on 23 November 1916 at the age of 25.[230] On her death certificate there were two causes of death noted. One was cardiac arrest of one hour's duration and the other was leprosy of six years duration.[231] She was buried in the Peel Island

---

[228] 'Finger, Hilda 1916', viewed 5/12/2023 https://www.findagrave.com/memorial/184665842/hilda-finger?...

[229] 'HIV.gov: A Timeline of HIV and AIDS', viewed 3/01/2023 https://www.hiv.gov/hiv-basics/overview/history/hiv-and-aids-timeline#year-1981

[230] Mackay Family History Society, 2012, 'Hilda Finger: Tailoress 1891', op. cit.

[231] *Deaths in the District of Brisbane in the State of Queensland: Hilda Finger*, 1916, Brisbane, The Government.

cemetery in an unmarked grave. Noel Flor, her nephew, commented that the 'white' male and female patients were segregated on the Island. The 'white' patients were housed in sturdy huts on the Island whereas the 'coloured' patients were housed in huts with thatched roofs. On Sunday the men and women would attend a church service in the morning and in the afternoon, they were free to mingle and play tennis. Visitors were few. Finger became friendly with a young male patient and formed a relationship with him. It was suggested that on hearing of his death, she had a heart attack and died. On visiting the Island, Flor could not find his aunt's grave because a bushfire had burnt the wooden crosses that marked the graves, so her burial location is unknown.[232]

Events:
- 1910 Diagnosed with Leprosy
- 1911 Arrived at Peel Island, Moreton Bay Leprosarium

Figure 24 Steamer *Porpoise* with wooden crate leaving Port of Mackay. Photograph courtesy of Mackay Family History Society.

---
[232] Flor, Noel, op. cit.

Finlay, Mary, Miss (1886-1966)

Figure 25 Miss Mary Finlay in 1937.
Photograph courtesy of Mackay Regional Council Libraries Heritage Collection, *Daily Mercury* Archive.

Born:
- 27 June 1886
- Mackay, Queensland, Australia

Died:
- 22 January 1966
- Mackay, Queensland. She was buried at Mount Bassett Cemetery.

Occupation:
- Clerk and Tailoress, Finlay was the first female alderman on the Mackay City Council. She was also a Justice of the Peace for Queensland and New South Wales, as well as Deputy Chairman of the Mackay Hospital Board, a Labourite and Hibernian.

Summary:

Mary Finlay was born in Mackay to James and Julia McDonald Finlay. She had one brother, Bernard Joseph who was also an alderman on the Mackay City Council. Mary lived with her parents in Gregory Street until later in life when she moved to Alfred Street, Mackay. He father was a nightwatchman and her mother a dressmaker. Finlay's first career was that of a tailoress before gaining employment with the Australian Workers Union (AWU) in Mackay as a clerk for twenty-seven years. She became assistant secretary and was associated with the Australian Labor Party for thirty-nine years.[233]

In her 50s, Finlay was appointed as a replacement to fill a vacancy on the Mackay City Council caused by the resignation of Jack Binnington in August 1937, a position she held for twenty-two months. 'Although she was not the first woman to serve on a Queensland local authority, she had the distinction of being the first female alderman, and the first woman to become a member of a city corporation in the state.'[234]

Finlay had many and varied interests. She believed that there was a real need for more women to serve on public boards and demonstrated her beliefs by becoming one of the few women in the state to serve on a city council. She topped the poll to become an alderman in the Mackay Town Council elections of 1937. She was the only female member of the Mackay Hospital Board. Her association with the hospital lasted for twenty-three years. One of her achievements was to convince the board to appoint a housekeeper, a role she regarded as essential for the wellbeing of hospital staff and patients.

Another achievement was that of chairman of the parks and reserves committee contributing to the establishment of Mackay's parks, public gardens, tree-shaded streets and pensioners' reserve.

---

[233] 'Honoured by A.W.U. Tribute to Miss Finlay', 1952, *Daily Mercury*, Tuesday 29 January, p.2.
[234] 'Woman as Mackay City Councillor: Miss Mary Finlay Appointed', 1937, *The Courier-Mail*, Friday 27 August 1937, p.14.

'The establishment of an old age pensioners' reserve has provided aged people with an area where they can build small homes, secure water and light services, and cultivate both vegetable and flower gardens.'[235] The hard work of setting up the gardens was completed for the pensioners' which meant they could be involved in less arduous tasks. As well as her political associations, Finlay spent twenty years as secretary of the Ladies Hibernian Society.

On the political front, Finlay was an excellent organiser as demonstrated when she organised candidates for the 1931 Mackay City Council elections. At the time she was campaign manager for the Labor Party. She successfully returned a full Labor Council.

Finlay was also campaign secretary for the Premier, Forgan Smith, during his election campaigns. She commented to the *Daily Mercury* when nearing retirement that she would deeply regret severing her relationship with the AWU because the office in Mackay was a second home to her.

> I have been mixed up in the hurly burly of political life ever since I can remember. In the early days of Mr Forgan Smith's career when he was winning his spurs as a politician, I was always his campaign director. As Mr Forgan Smith improved his status in the political life of the State, no one sat back and admired him more than I did. When he was elevated to Premier, I was thrilled, and anything I had done to put him into Parliament had been repaid handsomely.[236]

Finlay had maintained a close friendship with Forgan Smith over many years. She believed that ... 'he had done more for this city than any other public man in the last 25 years.'[237]

Finlay's employer at the AWU office commented at her retirement picnic that she had always been a loyal workmate, hardworking,

---

[235] 'Mackay Kens Miss Mary Finlay: Many Public Interests', 1938, *Queensland Country Life,* Thursday 21 July, p.7.

[236] 'After 27 Years Miss Finlay Retiring from A.W.U. Office', 1951, *Daily Mercury*, Friday 20 April 1951, p.2.

[237] ibid.

efficient and kind. 'I will miss her tremendously. I am pleased she will continue her interest in Labor activities after she terminates her long and devoted service with my union.'[238]

The farewell picnic for Finlay was held at Seaforth beach in January 1952. Over one hundred AWU convention delegates and local Australian Labor party members attended. She was presented with a silver tea and coffee service. The teapot contained some 'green tea' (cash) and a cheque as additional recognition for a lifetime of faithful service.[239] Finlay died at Mackay on 26 January 1966 at the age of 79 years.

Events:

- 1931 Organised Labor candidates for Mackay City Council elections
- 1935 Clerk Australian Workers Union Mackay
- 1937 Alderman Mackay City Council
- 1952 Retired

Figure 26 Miss Mary Finlay and Mackay City Council Aldermen in 1937. Photograph courtesy of Mackay Regional Council Libraries Heritage Collection, *Daily Mercury* Archive.

---

[238] 'Honoured by A.W.U. Tribute to Miss Finlay', op. cit., p.2.
[239] ibid.

Fudge, Naomi (1864-1946)

Figure 27 Naomi Fudge. Photograph courtesy of the Penny family.

Born:
- 11 July 1864
- Yeovil, South Somerset District, Somerset England

Died:
- 31 January 1946
- Mater Hospital, Mackay, Queensland

Occupation:
- Secretary, Australian Workers Union, grazier/farmer, caterer and undertaker. Fudge adapted to life in Australia in difficult circumstances, created a life for her family and contributed to her local community.

Alternative name/s:
- Naomi Hooper

Summary:

Naomi and Albert John Wellman Fudge immigrated to Australia in 1884, after they married in Yeovil, Somerset, England at the Baptist Church Yeovil, 27 December 1882. They sailed from London aboard the *Duke of Buccleuch*, on 31 December 1884, disembarking in Brisbane on 25 February 1885, later sailing onto Townsville.[240]

Fudge's parents were Samuel and Jane Hooper also of Somerset. Her husband, Albert, was also born in Yeovil on 30 January 1858. He was a 'bounty immigrant', a person sponsored by a colonist who employed him. The sponsor would then be reimbursed by the government. His migrant obligations were fulfilled when he worked as a carpenter on the Hamley Plantation near Townsville for twelve months.[241] He also had brick masonry and plumbing skills.

Their first child, Louis Robert was born in Ingham in 1886, where the Fudges worked on a tin mine at Kangaroo Hills. Knowledge of tin mining came with Albert from his home county in England. Their son was the first white child to be born on the tin fields and was reported to have caused a stir amongst the local Indigenous population.[242] Presumably, this was their first glimpse of a white baby. Conditions on the tin fields were described as 'primitive'. The heavy wet season made the beds of the creeks unworkable, and the range was described as inaccessible. Horses were the mode of transport, and people camped in rough precipitous country. There were two stores and a butchery at the main camp.[243]

The family relocated to Townsville where Albert Fudge gained employment as a carpenter with Burns Philp and Company. At

---

[240] 'Naomi Hooper', 2023, viewed 2023-08-08 http://www.ancestry.com.au
[241] Smith, Graham, [199?], 'Naomi and Albert John Wellman Fudge of Yeolands', [Mirani, Queensland], p.1.
[242] ibid., p.1.
[243] 'Kangaroo Hills Tin Mines', 1887, *Brisbane Courier*, Saturday 28 May, p.3. viewed 14/08/2023, http://nla.gov.au/nla.news-article3470567

this time, they lived on Ross Island for over two years, until 1889. It was here that their three daughters were born, Kate Elizabeth, Margaret and Agnes Jane. Further employment was found with the maritime engineering firm of J Vidulich and Company to build facilities at the Port of Townsville which lasted until 1893 when an opportunity arose to build a wharf and sheds on the Pioneer River at Mackay for the Adelaide Steamship Company. Fudge and the children remained in Townsville until 1894 when they joined Albert at Byron Street, Mackay.[244]

The family took up a selection of land the following year at Benholme, near Mirani in Naomi's name called 'Yeolands'. Albert built a home for them where they remained for over fifty years. Fudge bought land from the neighbours (Dan Ross, Christie Blum and William Jenner's 'Horse Ridge' farm)[245] and a herd of cattle numbering around two hundred. She had a small dairy built under the house and often worked outdoors, including the ring barking of trees with an axe. She also became secretary for the local branch of the Australian Worker's Union. A labour hall was built at Dow's Creek for such purposes which was demolished by the 1918 cyclone. She catered for many functions held in local halls to support community events. Naomi was instrumental in establishing a cemetery at Mirani West.[246]

Her husband Albert built the coffins (without nails) and she would lay-out the bodies for burial.[247] Fudge was a resourceful woman who once had to deal with the horse thief Columbus (Laudnagup)[248] who visited her on a stolen horse and demanded food, a saddle and a rope. Constable Archie McBride of Mirani

---

[244] Smith, Graham, op. cit., p.1.
[245] ibid., p.2.
[246] ibid.
[247] Gcasandra, 2018, '10 Pioneering Women Who Shaped Mackay's Future', *The Courier Mail*, viewed 14/04/2023 https://www.couriermail.com.au
[248] Fanning, Leonie, 2018, 'First Mirani Police Officer Attacked by a Horse Thief', *Townsville Bulletin*, January 3, p.2., viewed 18/08/2023 http://www.townsvillebulletin.com.au

was seriously wounded by Columbus wielding a sheath knife during his capture at Eungella. Columbus was later charged with horse stealing and attempted murder of First-Class Constable McBride. Constable McBride was commended and promoted for his bravery.[249]

The family increased in number with two sons being born at Yeolands, William (Bill) Vernon and Edgar. They also fostered Harry (Henry) Albert Penny the youngest son of a neighbour, whose mother Elizabeth, had died birthing Harry. The Pennys were a large family of seven children. Relatives of the Penny's described how Fudge went to the property next door and said, "give the baby to me'. She took him home and brought him up as a member of the Fudge family. Brian Penny, son of Harry, described how close they were to the Fudge family. The Pennys still call the Fudge family members Uncle and Aunt.[250]

The two sons who enlisted in World War I were; Edgar, who was killed at Hessian Wood, France, aged 21 years in 1918; and Louis Robert (a railway engine driver) who served with the Australian Infantry Force (AIF), in France. Another son, Bill Vernon became a schoolteacher and was well-known throughout Queensland. Following the First World War, the Fudge family were busy planting memorial trees in Mirani, the last tree that was planted was in memory of their son Edgar. Catherine Fudge married Charles Williamson, railway examiner who lived in Mackay. Agnes Jane married A H (Sonny) Brownsey of Elliot Grove and Margaret became a schoolteacher and married Alex Johnston a butcher from Sarina.[251]

Albert Fudge sought election to State Parliament as the Member for Mackay and was successful defeating David Dalrymple in a close ballot. He served for three years and did not seek re-election

---

[249] 'Telegrams', 1903, *North Queensland Register*, Monday 13 July, p.6. viewed 15/08/2023 http://nla/gov/au/nla-news-article84414849
[250] Penny, Brian, 2023, *Interview*, Mackay, 2/06/2023.
[251] Smith, Graham, op. cit., p.3.

because he did not enjoy political life. He went on to invent agricultural equipment for the sugarcane industry including the popular cane lift, ably assisted by Harry Penny. He designed and supervised construction of the footbridge attached to the Mirani railway bridge.[252]

Naomi Fudge lived until 82 years and 6 months, having lived in Queensland for sixty years. She died in 1946 and was buried in the Mackay City Cemetery. Her husband Albert, lived to the age of 91 and was buried with his wife.

Events:

- 1885 Arrived in Australia from Somerset, England
- 1894 Arrived in Mackay

Figure 28 The Fudge family L-R Front row: Edgar, Naomi (Grandma), Harry Penny (foster son), Albert (Grandpa) and William.
L-R Back row: Agnes, Louis, Catherine, Margaret. Photograph courtesy of the Penny family.

---

[252] Laskey, Alan, 2017, 'The Fudges of Yeolands', *Daily Mercury*, March 9, p.13.

Glenny, Ethel Victoria Octavia (1878-1962)

Figure 29 Ethel Victoria Octavia Cook Glenny. Photograph courtesy of Greenmount Historic Homestead collection circa 1919.

Born:
- 14 April 1878
- Balnagowan, Mackay district, Queensland.

Died:
- 1 September 1962
- Palm Beach, Northern Beaches, New South Wales (NSW)

Occupation:
- Socialite, artist, grazier and traveller. Glenny followed the lifestyle of her family and travelled extensively.

Alternative name/s:
- Ethel Cook, Babs

Summary:

Ethel Victoria Octavia was the youngest daughter of John and Elizabeth Cook of Balnagowan near Mackay. A separate entry has been written for Elizabeth Cook. The children were taught at home by Elizabeth until they reached secondary education level when both Cook and her brother Albert were taught by George Perkins, (who had matriculated from Oxford University), at his private school in Mackay. Perkins had arrived in Australia in 1883. There was not a state education system in the Mackay district at that time. It was at Perkins Private School that the Cook children were to meet the Atherton children.[253] It was at this private school that Cook met Vida Althaea Atherton. The two girls went on to become good friends and sisters-in-laws later in life. Cook exhibited her artwork at the Royal Art Society of New South Wales as E Cook in 1885 and 1886.[254]

Cook continued her education at the Armidale Presbyterian Ladies College in the 1890s. Following her school days, she became an inveterate traveller. She went to Port Hedland by steamer with her sister Cecilia (Cissy) after the birth of Cissy's son Frank in 1898.[255] She again travelled by steamer to England in 1907 returning via Java and calling in to see sister Cissy at Port Hedland. Inclement weather delayed her coming out of Java on the way to Australia, and she missed her brother Albert's wedding to Vida Atherton in 1908.

Another trip by steamer to England, this time in search of family history records in Cornwall, was undertaken and she again visited Europe in 1909. A visit to Blackheath and Jenolan Caves in New South Wales with visits in between to the family residence (Uncle Thomas's estate) at Turanville, Scone where she resided for twelve

---

[253] Clark, Betty, 1992, *A House Well Filled*, Mackay, Mackay Printing & Publishing, p.24.
[254] Christine Feher, Secretary, Royal Art Society, New South Wales, 2024, 27 August, confirmed in an email.
[255] Clark, Betty, op. cit., p.63.

months, occurred in 1910. Again, she travelled to England with her sisters Florence (Flo) and Isabel in 1914 and they remained there for the period of the war. Distance and slow transport did not seem to deter Cook form her travels. Travel, it would seem, was a replacement for a career that Ethel either did not have the opportunity to achieve or for which she did not aspire.

The marriage of Ethel Cook and Major Thomas Alexander Glenny took place at St Pancras, London on 15 April 1915. Major Glenny's military unit was the King's Own Scottish Borderers. Unfortunately, Major Glenny was killed in action in September 1915 before he met his baby son, Dennis Ross who was born in London in 1916.[256] Glenny returned to Australia and lived in New South Wales until she died in 1962.

Events:

- 1883 Tuition from the George Perkins Private School, Mackay
- 1890s Attended Armidale Presbyterian Ladies College, New South Wales
- 1914 Lived in London.
- 1916 Returned to Australia

---

[256] ibid., p. 39.

Insch, Margaret Mitchell (1854-1944)

Figure 30 Margaret Insch
Photograph courtesy of the Pioneer Valley Museum.

Born:
- 3 September 1854
- Longside, Aberdeenshire, Scotland

Died:
- 9 January 1944
- Mackay region, Queensland

Occupation:
- Midwife, and the first Northern European woman to cross the range by Carl Flor's track. Insch delivered ninety-nine babies as a local midwife in the Mirani district.

Alternative Name/s:
- Margaret Mitchell Milne, 'Granny' Insch

Summary:

Margaret Milne was one of several children born to Alexander and Catherine Milne (formerly Bruce) in 1854. Her father (a general labourer) remarried after her mother died in 1876 and had another four children. Milne found employment as a domestic servant by the age of 15 in Aberdeenshire. Her first child, Catherine (Kate) Milne Insch, was born in 1874 at Fetterangus, Old Deer, Aberdeenshire) followed by the birth of James Milne Insch in March of 1876. Unfortunately, James died in October of the same year. Alexander Insch was born in October of 1879, followed by Eliza Robertson Insch in October 1879. All the children were born at Fetterangus, Old Deer, Aberdeenshire. Milne, at the age of 25 in 1879 married Alexander Robertson Insch, a farm servant from Newton on Hythie, Old Deer, Aberdeenshire. Alexander was born on 27 January 1856 at Longside, Aberdeenshire. They exchanged banns according to the forms of the Established Church of Scotland.[257] Again, it was unfortunate to lose another child when Eliza died in July of 1882.

The Insch family, Alexander, Margaret, Kate and Alexander (junior) sailed from Glasgow, Scotland to Mackay,[258] Queensland on board the ship *Scottish Wizard*, on 4 June 1883.[259] The voyage took several months. During the voyage nine babies were born and there were eleven burials at sea. On arrival at Mackay all immigrants were domiciled at the immigration depot in Tennyson Street. There were no beds available, so they slept on the floor of the Depot for three weeks, plagued by mosquitos.[260] A sister to Alexander Insch, Ann, also travelled with the family as did Margaret's brother John Milne.

---

[257] Extract of an Entry in a Register of Marriage, 1879, 'A Insch and Margaret Milne', Edinburgh, Scotland, viewed 20/04/2023 https://www.ancestry.com.au

[258] 'Shipping', *Brisbane Courier*, 1883, Monday 18 June, p.1., viewed 2023-04-26 Http://nla.gov.au

[259] *Scottish Wizard: Passenger List*, 1883, Archives Queensland, 2023 email confirmed info@archives.qld.gov.au, 20 April 2023.

[260] Laskey, Alan, 2017, 'Pioneering Granny Insch Forged a Long Life in the Valley', viewed 2023-04-20 https://www.ancestry.com.au

Alexander Insch found work as a stableman at Te Kowai, and they pitched a tent on the riverbank until they found a house. The roads in those days were bush tracks. The Insch family took up a selection on the Hamilton Run, across the Pioneer River from Mirani. Insch kept a black book in which she recorded marriages, births, accidents, deaths and social events about many Pioneer Valley residents.[261]

Another son, George, was born in August of 1883 - two months after they arrived in Mackay - followed by James Florence in January in 1885, William in October of 1886 and John Milne Insch in November of 1888 and David McClure Insch born in November of 1880. James Florence died of tuberculosis (known as phthisis) in July of 1891 and William died from a kick by a horse in July 1892 at Dimbulah.[262] A son, Edward Blann[263] was born in September of 1893 and another baby was stillborn in 1895 when Insch was 41 years old. The family adopted or fostered a daughter, Bella. That gave them twelve children. It was reported Insch adopted the girl 'to make up a foot, she said.'[264]

Towards the end of 1889, Alexander, Alexander (junior) and Frank Douglas were the first Europeans to cut their way through the bush to the foot of the Eungella range at the time of the Eungella gold diggings. They reached their destination on the third day having lost several horses over the side of the steep range. Two tents were erected with one for the family, and the other for goods carted from Mirani and carried over the range by horses to the diggings. Insch was the first European woman to cross the range by Carl Flor's track. 'On one occasion, in order to contact her

---

[261] ibid.
[262] Mackay Family History Society, 2009. 'Alexander Insch', *Early Settlers of Mackay 1860-1885*, Mackay, The Society, p.444.
[263] Edward Blann Insch enlisted in the Light Horse (5th AIF) in World War I and although wounded, he served in World War II as a Warrant Officer. He was mentioned in dispatches. National Archives of Australia, viewed 2023-04-18 https://www.ancestry.com.au
[264] Mackay Family History Society, op. cit., p.444.

husband, she was forced to crawl on her hands and knees with her four-year-old George by her side.'²⁶⁵ During the time they were seeking gold, she ran a boarding house at the foot of Eungella range.²⁶⁶

Insch was known by most people in the district for her many good deeds of mercy. An uncle in Scotland, who was a doctor, passed onto her his skills before she immigrated to Australia. There were not many doctors available in the early days of settlement, so Insch provided aid for those in need. When the creeks and rivers were flooded, she would go out to visit people at any time of day or night to bring relief to their suffering. 'Granny' a former midwife, delivered ninety-nine babies, and it is reported she said, 'It ought to have been another one to make a hundred.'²⁶⁷

A venture into the sugar cane industry at Eton, was followed by the family returning to their home at Hamilton. Alexander then disposed of the property to David McClure. He took up part of Hollow Estate, known as Sunnyside. Alexander died at Sunnyside at age 49 in July of 1905. Insch worked the property for several years prior to living at Mirani in Maud Street. When ill-health prevailed, after living for thirty years in Mirani, she moved into Mackay to live with a granddaughter. She died on 9 January 1944 aged 89 years. Both Alexander and 'Granny' Insch are buried in Mirani West Cemetery.

Events:

- 1883 Arrived in Mackay
- 1883 Midwife in Mackay district
- 1889 First woman to cross Eungella range by Carl Flor's track and managed a boarding house

---

[265] Laskey, Alan, op. cit.
[266] Mackay Family History Society, 2009, op. cit., p.444.
[267] Pioneer Valley Museum, 2018, 'Alexander and Granny Insch', Mirani, The Museum, p. [1].

Links:

Gcasandra, 2018, '10 Pioneering Women who Shaped Mackay's Future', *The Courier Mail*, viewed 2023-04-14 https://www.couriermail.com.au/news/queensland/mackay/

Figure 31 Granny Insch
Photograph courtesy of the Pioneer Valley Museum.

Kemmis, Emily Slatyer (abt.1845-1913)

**Figure 32 Emily Slatyer Gibson.
Photograph courtesy of Mackay Family History Society.**

Born:
- abt 1845
- Jamaica

Died:
- 22 August 1913
- Roseville, Yass Valley Council, New South Wales

Occupation:
- Educator and farmer - Kemmis established the first indepentent school in the Mackay district.

Alternative Name/s:
- Emily Slatyer Gibson

Summary:

Arriving in Australia with her family in 1850, Emily Slayter Gibson, born in Jamaica about 1845, was the only daughter of Reverend John Gibson and Mary Jane Simpson Todd. The family lived in Grafton for three years during which time her mother and three brothers died from gastric fever. Her father remarried and together with his new wife, took Emily and two remaining brothers and moved to Newcastle. Later they moved to Campbelltown. It was during her father's absence in England that Gibson married Arthur Alexander Kemmis at Campbelltown, New South Wales, on 2 June 1864.[268] Arthur had already travelled north to the new township of Mackay and brought Emily back with him. He was a widower as his first wife, Jessie Holmes[269], had died at the age of 20.[270]

The Kemmis family were some of the first settlers in Mackay and lived in Varroville on Nebo Road. They had twelve children: Mary Aphrasia May (May) born 2 May 1865; Arthur Hume Raymond (Ray) born in 20 July 1866; Florence Emily Maria born in 16 April 1868; Ernest Sidney born in 13 January 1870; Cecil Frank (Nipper) born 28 October 1871; Amy born in 20 September 1873; Ida Myrza born in 4 July 1875; Vivien Maughan (Jack) born 14 February 1877; Lionel de Camois born 11 February 1879; Ruby Muriel born 9 March 1881; Cyril Guy born 15 October 1883; and Gerald Wilfred born 7 May 1887.[271]

By 1872, the Kemmis family had taken up 365 acres of pastoral land at Oakenden. It is believed that the house named 'Oakenden' meant 'a den among the wild oaks' referring to the oaks that grew profusely along the creek banks. In the early 1880's, the family

---

[268] 'Emily S Gibson', 1864, *Australian Marriage Index 1788-1950*, viewed 5/05/2023 https://www.ancestry.com.au/search/collections/1780/records/1754626
[269] 'Arthur Kemmis (1834-1896)', 2022, Genealogy, viewed 5/01/2023 https://www.geni.com/people/Arthur-Kemmis/6000000007779774213
[270] Mackay Family History Society, 2012, 'Emily Kemmis', Mackay, The Society.
[271] 'Arthur Kemmis (1834-1896)', 2022, op. cit.

moved further down Broadsound Road to a property that they called 'The Chase'.[272]

Kemmis, who was well educated herself, was not happy sending her children to the Homebush School established in 1889, so she engaged a tutor and opened a private boarding house at her home. The tutor taught Latin, Greek classics, Mathematics, French, Geography, English, commercial subjects, music and drawing. The girls were also taught needlework. Kemmis advertised classes in the *Daily Mercury* for a fee of 50 guineas per year.[273]

Around 1895, Kemmis and her husband relocated to Sydney. Kemmis died on 22 August 1913 and is buried at Rookwood Cemetery with her husband.[274]

Events:

- 1850 Arrived in Sydney from Jamaica
- 1864 Arrived in Mackay
- 1872 Purchased Oakenden Estate
- 1880s Purchased the Chase, further down Broadsound Road
- 1880s Established a boarding school
- 1893 Moved to Sydney

---

[272] Mackay Family History Society, 2012, 'Emily Kemmis', op. cit.
[273] ibid.
[274] ibid.

**Figure 33 Kemmis family Mackay 1895.
Photograph courtesy of *Ancestry.com.au***

**Back row: Cecil Frank Kemmis, Ida Myrza Conolly (Kemmis),
Lionel de Camois Kemmis**

Second row: Amy Constance Bellamy Jordan (Kemmis), Arthur Hume Raymond (Ray) Kemmis, Emily Slatyer Kemmis (Gibson), Vivian Maughan (Jack) Kemmis, Ruby Muriel Fyson Murray (Kemmis)

Front row: Cyril Kemmis, Gerald Wilfred Vincent Kemmis (missing are Ernest Sidney, Mary Aphrasia (May) Fenner (Kemmis), Florence Emily Ninna Farquhar (Kemmis), and Arthur Alexander Kemmis

Knezevic, Catherine Ann Stevenson (1957-2022)

Figure 34 Cathy Knezevic. Photograph courtesy of *Mackay and Whitsunday Life*, 2023.

Born:
- 26 November 1957
- Mackay, Queensland

Died:
- 14 August 2022.
- Mackay, Queensland

Occupation:
- Library assistant, art assistant, home decorator and business woman Cathy utilised her artistic talents to involve others and to create and promote interest in artistic décor, works of art, writers and art feativals in Mackay and the Whitsundays.

Alternative Name/s:
- Cathy Stevenson, Cathy Phillips, Cathy Casey.

Summary:

Cathy Stevenson was one of five children born to Brian Desmond and Antionette (Toni) Mifsud Stevenson. She was the eldest daughter, having one sister and three brothers. Her father was a cane cutter and later a farmer working and living in the Walkerston district. Stevenson had a romantic encounter at the age of 15. Her first son Adam was the outcome of that union. He was adopted out and later in life met up with his mother. Stevenson went on to marry Ian Phillips with whom she had another son Ben. After divorcing Phillips, she met and married George Knezevic with whom she had Emma and Adam. Her later partner for twenty years was the award-winning carpenter, Tom Casey.

Geraldine Moylan (former Chief Librarian) commented that Knezevic during her early career, was employed as a part-time library assistant on contract by the Mackay Regional Library service for approximately twenty years and subsequently worked as a contract part-time assistant exhibition officer at Artspace Mackay for the Mackay Regional Council. (MRC).

After leaving the MRC, Knezevic operated Arthouse Gallery, a private art gallery she established at 148 Wood Street, Mackay.[275] Knezevic did attend some art classes offered by Clem Forbes, a prominent artist and educator in the Mackay district during the 1990s. Leoni Wood who became friends with Knezevic, was one of the eleven local female artists linked through Forbes's drawing classes. The other ten were, Kay Brampton, Mary Brown, Margaret Burgess, Irene Coburn, Alison Fenech, Lesley Kane, Lyn Laver Ahmat, Maria Lenz, Sybil Rodger and Raye Williams.[276]

Knezevic's partner of twenty years was Casey with whom she contributed her interior design skills to decorate the many buildings that they renovated and built. Casey was named National Carpenter of the Year in 2009 for his skills not only as a carpenter but for his community work as a member of the Mackay Regional Council's

---

[275] Moylan, Geraldine, 2024, *Interview*, 5/07/2024.
[276] 'Forged by Forbes and Friendship', 2024, viewed 5/07/2024 https://www.mackay.qld.gov.au/about_council/news_and_media...

Heritage Advisory Committee. He was instrumental in his fundraising efforts to restore St Pauls Uniting Timber Church in Mackay.[277] The Queensland Master Builders Association now offers the Tom Casey Award for a new or refurbished heritage home.

Arthouse Gallery was relocated from Wood Street in Mackay to underneath the house she shared with Casey in Walkerston and then subsequently moved to Airlie Beach. In 2019 she met Jessica Begun, patron of this year's Whitsundays Writers Festival, and suggested they combine their skills and launched the inaugural Whitsundays Arts festival in September 2020.[278]

Tragically, Knezevic was diagnosed with stage four cancer at the time she received the news that they were successful in gaining funding for the inaugural arts festival. The second and third festivals continued to expand with a focus on multicultural performances, stories and a film screening in Proserpine. She continued to battle cancer and lived to enjoy the second festival with her whole family. Her legacy lives on through the dedication of Begun and other volunteers.

Knezevic died in 2022 and was buried at Walkerston Cemetery. Wood remembers her as a 'down to earth person', who had a 'wicked sense of humour.'[279] She took the opportunity to contribute her many talents to the community and those around her.

Events:

- 2019 Moved to Airlie Beach
- 2019 Whitsunday Writers Festival
- 2020 Whitsunday Arts Festival

Links:

MackayandWhitsundayLifehttps://www.mackayandwhitsundaylife.com/article/a-great-light-now-soars

---

[277] Jacques, Owen, 2009, *The Courier Mail*, June 26, viewed 6/07/2024 https://www.couriermail.com.au/news/queensland/mackay

[278] Hutchings, Melinda Louise, 2024, 'A Creative Mind: Jess Begun, Patron of the Whitsundays Writers Festival', *Whitsunday Life*, Friday 5 July, p.24.

[279] Wood, Leoni, 2024, *Interview*, 5/07/2024.

Koch, Maria Verena (1844-1937)

Figure 35 Maria Verena Koch. Photograph Courtesy *Ancestry.com.au*.

Born:
- 1844
- Baden, Switzerland

Died:
- 19 February 1937
- Mater Hospital, Mackay, Queensland

Occupation:
- Farmer, horse-woman, early settler, a focal point for the local community and friend to Pacific Islanders.

Alternative Name/s:

- Mary Koch, Maria Verena Meyer, Maria Verona Meier, Mary Virginia Koch, Granny Koch.

Summary:

Maria Verena Meyer was born in Baden, a town in Switzerland, 25 km northwest of Zurich, to parents Joseph Meyer and Maria Burger. She left her homeland for Australia at age 26 in 1870 during the time of the Franco-Prussian War. She recalled seeing the trainloads of prisoners of war when she passed through Germany. As an assisted migrant, she boarded the sailing ship *Gutenburg* in December 1970 from Hamburg in Germany, sailing to Keppel Bay arriving on 24 March 1871. A journey of three months. It was not only a long arduous journey, but on arrival there was not adequate infrastructure and services for immigrants at Keppel Bay. She resided at Rockhampton for nine months prior to travelling to Mackay.[280]

Meyer married Joseph Fredrich Koch, a blacksmith, in Mackay on 9 January 1873. His parents were Martin Koch and Agetha Kaniber of Griessau, Lechtal, Tyrol (Tirol), Austria. Koch immigrated from Hamburg, Germany to Australia aboard the sailing ship *La Rochelle*, arriving in Moreton Bay 5 August 1865. Father Bacus, a well-known local Catholic priest, performed the marriage ceremony. He became a lifelong friend of the family. The couple had six children - five daughters and one son; Mary Josephine Koch White (1873-1945); a daughter (Julia Mary 1875-1882) who died at the age of seven; Mary Selina Koch Macartney (1877-1958); Amelia Koch 'Millie' (1880-1933); Mary Ludwina Koch Howell (1884-1981); and William Francis Joseph 'Bill' Koch (1886-1957). Bill Koch enlisted in both World Wars.[281] He was in the 11th Light Horse Regiment, Australian Infantry Forces (AIF) in the First World War and enlisted in the Second World War one day earlier than his 56th birthday.[282]

---

[280] Mackay Family History Society, 2012, 'Mary Koch Farmer 1872', Mackay, The Society.

[281] *Deaths in the District of Mackay in the State of Queensland*, 1937, 'Mary Verena Koch', Mackay, Queensland, viewed 3/04/2023 https://www.qld.gov.au/law/births-deaths-marriages-and-divorces

[282] Koch, William Francis Joseph, 1914, Mackay, Queensland, viewed 4/05/2023 https://recordsearch.naa.gov.au/SearchNRetrieve/Interface/DetailsReports/ItemDetail.aspx?Barcode=7370897&isAv=N

The couple took up a selection of land at Slade Point which they sold a few years later to establish their property at Mount Cook, near Wundaru, located between Coningsby and Farleigh in the Mackay district. Koch ran the farm (for thirty-eight years), after the death of her husband Joseph on 17 June 1899 until son William came home from the war/s. As she aged, she became known as 'Granny Koch'. She had four surviving children after her death, nineteen grandchildren and ten great-grandchildren. When she was younger, she was a competent horsewoman. 'At one time, when wishing to return home to her baby, she, with her good horse, swam the river at the site where the hospital now stands. (There had been heavy rain while she was in Mackay and the river was rising. She could not swim, but rode the horse into the water, slipped off its back and held onto its tail while it swam across.)[283]

The family property at Mount Cook was renowned for its hospitality to passing visitors and locals alike. Koch gave aid to those who sought it especially in times of sickness and stress. She was well known to the other early settlers. For those who were having difficulty, the advice was 'Go to Granny Koch – she will help you'. Koch was a regular Roman Catholic Church goer and could be seen sitting in Jubilee Park at 5.30 am telling her beads prior to attending the church service. She was reputedly a good reader and had a good memory of the early days in Mackay when there was a few shacks and dense scrub in Sydney Street, Mackay. She was also a good friend to the Pacific Islanders in the district. Maria Koch died at the age of 93 on the February 1937 and was buried at the Mackay City Cemetery.[284]

Events:

- 1871 Arrived in Queensland
- 1873 Farmer

---

[283] 'The Passing of a Pioneer', 1937, *Daily Mercury*, Friday 26, p.9. viewed 9/02/2024, http://nla.gov.au/nla.news-article170261896
[284] Mackay Family History Society, 2012, 'Mary Koch Farmer 1872' op. cit.

McBurney, Maria Emma (1849-1935)

Figure 36 Maria Emma McBurney, Wild Passionflower circa 1880. Photograph courtesy of Artspace Mackay.

Born:
- 24 May 1849
- Sydney, New South Wales

Died:
- 12 July 1935
- Ealing, London, England

Occupation:
- As an artist and writer, McBurney painted the local flora especially wildflowers of the Mackay district leaving a realistic record of the local native vegetation for future generations to admire.

Alternative Name/s:
- Maria Emma Palmer, Emma McBurney

Summary:

An outstanding Australian artist of the nineteenth century, Maria Emma McBurney was the fourth daughter of Edward Thompson Palmer and Jane Emily Robinson Palmer. She had two brothers and five sisters. As wife to Dr Robert Campbell McBurney, Emma spent twenty-five years of her life in Mackay, from 1874 to 1899, except for the year 1884. Her husband was the first surgeon-superintendent of the Mackay District Hospital. Maria Emma McBurney, as she was known, married Dr Robert Campbell McBurney on 22 April 1974 at St Mary's Church in Kangaroo Point, Brisbane.[285]

Dr McBurney was born in Belfast, Ireland and trained at the Royal College of Physicians, Edinburgh, Scotland. He was the first resident medical officer in Mackay, arriving in 1869.[286] He had purchased about ten acres of land along Nebo Road Mackay, directly opposite what is now the Regional Botanic Gardens.

They named the residence 'Kaligul', referring to the Aboriginal name for the freshwater lagoon nearby. The building was unusual for those times with its high-blocked verandahs characterised by distinctive balustrading of a sunburst pattern, interspersed with panels of geometric design. A skillion kitchen was inside the building which was unusual for the times. The gable of the outside bathroom and servants' quarters featured a small dovecote (a shelter with nest holes for domestic pigeons). Cooling vines moderated the effects of the western sun.[287]

The McBurneys had two daughters, Laura Elizabeth born on 20 February 1877 and Rhoda Thompson born 11 December 1879 who died at Port Mackay in July of 1880 at 7 months.[288]

---

[285] 'Marriages, 1874, *The Sydney Morning Herald*, Friday June 19, p.8., https://www.ancestry.com.au/search/collections/9091/records/1590374658

[286] Clark, Betty, 1992, *A House Well Filled*, Mackay, Mackay Printing & Publishing, p. 23.

[287] *Mackay Regional Botanic Gardens Kaligul*, 2023, viewed 07/03/2023 https://www.mackayregionalbotanicalgardens.com.au

[288] 'Deaths', 1880, *Sydney Morning Herald*, Thursday 29 July, p.1., viewed 07/03/2023 http://nla.gov.au/nla.news-article13465029

Dr Robert and Emma McBurney with their daughter, travelled to England, Scotland and Ireland via the United States of America in 1884, returning to Mackay in December 1885. During their time in England, Emma staged an exhibition of her Mackay artwork which created a sensation amongst the English population, never having seen Australian fauna and flora depicted in such a way. The exhibition attracted Australian attention as well. The artist had also published a story *Tassong's Ghost, An Old Time Story of the North Queensland Cane Fields*, printed in 1915 to aid the Australian Red Cross.[289]

Following Robert McBurney's retirement from the Mackay District Hospital in October 1898, the McBurney's left town in January 1899, intending to settle in Sydney. Dr McBurney died suddenly in Apia, Western Samoa, while traveling to the USA as a ship's doctor. McBurney lived in Sydney, but also travelled to England where her daughter Laura Preedy was living. She died in London on 12 July 1935, aged 81-82 years.[290] She is buried in South Head Cemetery, Vaucluse, Waverly Council, New South Wales, Australia.

A collection of eight paintings by Emma McBurney, purchased in Rockhampton, was donated to Mackay City Council by Loraine and Simon McConnell in 1980, and are in the collection at Artspace Mackay. They depict flora of the Mackay district.

Events:

- 1874 Arrived in Mackay
- 1880 Completed notable art works
- 1884 Travelled overseas and exhibited artwork
- 1899 Relocated to Sydney

---

[289] McBurney, ME, 1915, *Tassong's Ghost, An Old Time Story of the North Queensland Cane Fields,* Melbourne, DW Paterson Company.
[290] Mackay Family History Society, 2012, 'Emma McBurney', Mackay, The Society.

Links:

Mackay Regional Botanical Gardens
https://mackayregionalbotanicalgardens.com.au

Figure 37 Maria Emma McBurney, Tropical Mushrooms circa 1880. Photograph courtesy of Mackay Regional Council, Artspace Mackay.

McDonald, Barbara (1869-1901)

Figure 38 Albion Hotel and Hall, Walkerston. Photograph courtesy of the State library of Queensland.

Born:
- 18 March, 1869
- Barry Brae, Aberdeenshire, Scotland, United Kingdom.

Died:
- 2 February 1901
- Walkerston, Mackay, Queensland

Occupation:
- Hotelier in the Mackay district from 1883-1901 and at the Albion Hotel, Walkerston from 1872-1901. MacDonald was a publican and her hotel was the centre of entertainment for the local district of Walkerston.

Alternative Name/s:
- Barbara Anderson

Summary:

Barbara Anderson was the daughter of Peter Anderson and Annie Jamieson, born in Barry Brae, Aberdeenshire, Scotland.[291] She was baptised there on 18 March 1829.[292] Scotland Census records indicate that Anderson worked as a female servant for two different families, the Farquhar family in 1841, and the Glennie family, in 1851.[293] It is believed that she arrived in Queensland during the 1860s. Passenger records for this period were damaged by the 1893 Brisbane floods.

At the age of 40, she married Archibald McDonald (who was four years younger and born in Nova Scotia, Canada, the son of Donald McDonald and Catherine Cameron), on 11 July 1869 at the house of James Greig at Lake Elphinstone. James Grieg was the publican of the Elphinstone Hotel at the time of the marriage (1863-1977).[294] Archibald, at the time of his marriage, was a sheep farmer at Lake Elphinstone. Lake Elphinstone is about 141 km southwest of Mackay.

The couple managed the Caledonian Hotel in Wood Street, later known as the Union Hotel before it was blown down during Cyclone Eline in 1898. The McDonalds managed the Caledonian from December 1869 until 1872. It was in November of 1872 that Archibald applied for a liquor license for a Walkerston building. He intended to name an existing building in Walkerston the Albion Hotel. This building contained three sitting rooms and four bedrooms as well as rooms for the McDonalds private use.

McDonald was at the age of 41 and 43, when she bore two sons, James Thomas Archibald (born 26 April 1870 and died 25

---

[291] NB: Brae is the Lowland Scots word for slope or brow of hill.
[292] Mackay Family History Society, 2012, 'Barbara McDonald: Hotelier 1869', Mackay, The Society.
[293] State Library of Queensland, 'Barbara McDonald', email ASK104043, 30 January 2024.
[294] Mackay Historical Society and Museum Inc., *Mackay Hotels A-K*, Mackay, viewed 12/1/2024 https://www.mackayhistory.org/research/hotels/hotels_a_to_k.html

September the same year) and James Donald (born 3 July 1871 and died 2 July 1872). Her husband Archibald succumbed to a fever of two weeks duration and died on 15 December 1872, at age 39 years.[295] He had lived in Australia for about nine years before his death and was buried in the Mackay Cemetery.

As a resourceful woman, McDonald applied for a transfer of her late husband's hotel license in January 1873 and built a new business in the form of a country pub.[296] This was not an easy task for a woman in colonial Queensland but soon the hotel began to prosper. There has been debate about whether there were two Albion Hotels on the site. Alec McColl uses the phrase 'the old Albion'. Jim Pascoe was credited with carting timber to build the Albion in 1881, and James Perry mentions 'Mrs McDonald of the original Albion Hotel.'[297] The second hotel, a larger structure, had iron-lace trim railings on the second level of the verandah. It was built in 1881.

McDonald was congratulated for her public spirit and local enterprise for erecting a large hall. Mackay Family History Society wrote that both the hotel and the hall were the pride of the district with people coming from all locations for a night of dancing on the hall's well-kept floor.[298] All were not impressed with the music coming from the hall and in 1874 RSP Brown, the publican of the other Walkerston hotel, the Alexandra, took the matter to court. The charge was that McDonald was in breach of the *Publican's Act* of 1863 by allowing music and dancing in the Albion Hotel on 15 February. Evidence was taken from three witnesses for the prosecution and two witnesses for the defence.

---

[295] Queensland Births, Deaths & Marriages, 1872, *Deaths in the District of Mackay in the Colony of Queensland*, Archibald Macdonald: Publican, Brisbane, BDM, viewed 12/01/2024, https://www.familyhistory.bdm.qld.gov.au/

[296] 'Advertising', 1873, *Mackay Mercury and South Kennedy Advertiser*, 18 January, viewed /1/2024, http://nla.gov/au/nla.news-article169703363

[297] Hamilton, Pat, 1994, *Sugar from the Scrub: A Pictorial History of Walkerston*, Mackay, Boolarong Press, p.41-42.

[298] *Mackay Family History Society*, 2012, *Barbara McDonald Hotelier 1869*, op. cit.

The finding was that 'The case was a most trumpery one and was in no way substantiated. The bench found a verdict for the defendant with costs.' [299]

McDonald became a well known and loved hostess as publican of the Albion for over thirty years, catering for many events such as balls, concerts, meeting and shows, starring overseas performers. On one such occasion in 1881, people were entertained by none other than Nellie Mitchell (who married Charles Nesbitt Frederick Armstrong in 1882), a local singer from Marian, later known internationally as Dame Nellie Melba. A Catholic Mass was first held in the hall in about 1880. Horse auctions during the 1880s drew large crowds of buyers. A St Patrick's Day ball was held in March of 1883 which was declared to be a huge success by the seventy-five couples who enjoyed an 'excellent supper.'[300]

MacDonald continued as owner of the Albion up until her death although she was assisted by managers. She died on 2 February 1901, aged 72 and is buried in the Walkerston Cemetery.

Events:
- 1869-1872 Caledonian Hotel Wood Street, Mackay
- 1873-1901 Albion Hotel, Walkerston

---

[299] 'Police Court – Mackay', 1874, *Mackay Mercury and South Kennedy Advertiser*, 28 February, p.2., viewed 5/1/2024, http://nla.gov.au/nla.news/news-article169859334

[300] Hamilton, Pat, op. cit.

Marlla, Katie (Kitty) (1860-1944)

Figure 39 Katie Marlla. Photograph courtesy of the Mackay Family History Society.

Born:
- Abt 1860
- Waluriki (Walarigi) Village, Ambae (Oba or Oboa) Island, Vanuatu[301]

Died:
- 16 July 1944
- Mackay, Queensland

---

[301] Ambae Island, also known as Aoba, Omba, Oba, or Opa, an island in the Vanuata archepelligo, was formerly a Lepers' Island, and periodically has volcanic ash eruptions from the Manaro Voui volcano.

Occupation:
- Sugarcane farmer, and Pacific Islander. Marlla suffered the trauma of being kidnapped as a young woman and lived to provide a life for herself and her family in Queensland.

Alternative Name/s:
- Katie (Kitty) Natofilinga or Natoflinga, Katie Malla or Katie Marella.

Summary:

Katie was born to Aron Natofilinga and an unknown mother in Waluriki Village on Ambae Island, Vanuatu. As a 15-year-old, in 1875, she and a female friend were kidnapped when walking along Wakurili beach to collect salt water for cooking in a 'bute', a bamboo water carrier. Two men had taken the girls from the beach in a rowboat out to the schooner *Borough Belle*.[302] They were not given the opportunity to tell their friends or family. The ship called in at many of the Pacific Islands[303] collecting mainly young men, to transport them to Australia for work in the sugarcane industry. During the voyage, they were assigned tasks, and the girls were given calico clothes and told to wash the deck down each day. The two girls had metal shackles placed around their ankles, the scars of which remained with them for life. For those who tried to escape once released from the hold, they were either captured, shot or when they tried to swim away, were taken by sharks. Natofilinga's female friend died during the voyage.

On arrival at Flat Top Island, Natofilinga was taken by Lighter to the mouth of the Pioneer River from where she walked in waist deep water to the river bank at Mackay and then onto Ashburton plantation.[304] The Pacific Islanders were then taken to cane farms in the region and assigned work in the fields.

---

[302] Mackay Family History Society, 2012, 'Katie Marlla', Mackay, The Society.

[303] Pacific Islanders were employed as indentured labourers in Australia, especially in the sugar and cotton plantations of Queensland. They were referred to as Kanakas.

[304] Trieve, Rowena, 1988, *Garden of Memories*, Mackay, The Author, [p.2].

Natofilinga first worked at Farleigh on a sugar plantation. She was taught how to plant and cut cane as well as housework for a meagre wage as an Indentured worker. Farm work consisted of clearing land on hillsides and working in cane fields. She worked for three decades in the fields before working in the homes of property owners, cooking and cleaning. Plantation owners could be strict and Katie 'had her ears boxed', and on one occasion she slept in the Mackay Cemetery.[305] Islanders were offered a free return passage to their homes after three years indenture to a property owner.

After twelve years, Natofilinga decided to take up the offer and returned to Oboa Island, Vanuatu accompanied by her eldest daughter, Rose Chole Tammar, on board the *'Jabberwalk'*. Rose was born in 1886 and later married Phillip Choppy on 18 September 1909.[306] Unfortunately, Natofilinga and her daughter were taken on a boat tour of the Torres Strait Islands, but were never taken to Vanautu.

Following her return to Australia, she worked at Alexandra, and it was at this plantation that she met a Fijian, Willie Marlla. They had two children, Irene (Ivy) (born 1904, who married William Thomas) and Alex (born 1907). Willie returned to Fiji in 1907 on the *Jabbowalk*, leaving the family behind. This was before Alex was born. Marlla then left Alexandra and began working for the Innes family who were kind to her. She then worked on a cattle property, where she was taught how to bake bread, cook and clean for a household and staff of fourteen. The Presbyterian Church Mission taught her to read and write as well as about spiritual matters.[307]

At the age of 67, in 1927, Marlla was not entitled to an age pension. She leased five acres of land on the side of Scrubby

---
[305] ibid., p.2.
[306] Rose Chole Tammar Choppy, 2023, *Find a Grave Memorial*, Mackay, State of Queensland, 'Births Deaths Marriages', viewed 2023-03-28 https://www.findagrave.com/memorial/199297449/
[307] Trieve, Rowena, op. cit., [p.5].

Mountain at Sunnyside. The land was cleared and sugarcane was planted by mattock and hoe. The variety of cane grown was Badilla and D1135. In the planting season, she would walk to a neighbouring farm owned by Harry Andrews at the 'Pocket', to obtain plants (having cut the stalks into short lengths). She carried them back to her plot in a sack, walking 14 miles home.[308] Every day, she would carry water in a kerosene tin, using a yoke across her shoulders, walking the two miles home. She worked her small farm for eleven years. Time had caught up with this courageous and determined little woman, and she spent her remaining years with her children.

Her long term friend, Lucy Querro, who was from the Solomon Islands, leased a cane farm at White Rocks Sunnyside near where Marlla had her farm.

Marlla was introduced to Christianity which became a very important part of her life. She would often quote many verses from her well-worn bible. The Islanders practiced traditions and customs of their homeland when first arriving in Australia and witchcraft was practised by some, although Christianity soon became the prevailing religion. Trieve mentioned that the Pacific Islanders from Obao strongly resented the use of the term 'Kanaka' because this was a derogatory term that meant 'a silly person' or a person of 'low standing' in the community.[309]

Despite the many hardships, Marlla overcame them and held the belief that Australia would provide many opportunities for her family. Today, the descendants of Katie Marlla reaped the benefits of her vision. She worked on farms in the Sarina and Homebush districts and encouraged her children to value education.[310]

One of her great-granddaughters was Gloria Arrow, the former housekeeper and caretaker of Greenmount Homestead in

---

[308] ibid.
[309] ibid.
[310] See entries for Gloria Arrow and Rowena Trieve OAM.

Walkerston. Arrow's grandmother was Rose Choppy, elder daughter of Katie Marlla. Marlla died on 16 July 1944 aged 83-84 years and is buried in Mackay Cemetery.[311] The descendants of Marlla compiled a booklet of their recollections in her honour, titled *Garden of Memories*.[312]

Events:

- 1875 Kidnapped (black birded) to work as an indentured labourer in the Queensland cane fields
- 1893 Returned to visit family in Vanuatu
- 1967 Purchased land for sugarcane farming

---

[311] ibid.
[312] Trieve, Rowena, op. cit., p.[1].

Marten, Annie Pring (1851-1933)

Figure 40 Winterbourne (Branscombe, home of Mr & Mrs G N Marten) 1873. Photograph courtesy of the Mackay Regional Council, Artspace Collection.

Born:
- 14 October 1851
- Kensington, London, England

Died:
- 8 January 1933
- St Albans, Herefordshire, England

Occupation:
- Water colour artist, painter and photographer. In the brief time Marten lived in Mackay, her art work became an important record of the life and times during early settlement.

Alternative Name/s:
- Annie Pring Taylor, Ann Pring Marten, Annie Marten, Ann Marten, Annie P Martin.

Summary:

Winterbourne Homestead, situated on the Branscombe Plantation, as painted by the new bride when she arrived in Queensland in 1873. Annie Pring Taylor married George Nisbet Marten at Marylebone Church in London 14 November 1872. George had purchased the 683-acre property with Edward Maitland Long in 1870. Taylor, the daughter of Harriett and John Taylor, was born in London England. George Nisbet (who became a first-class cricketer and banker) was the son of Thomas Powney Marten and Clara Elizabeth Nisbet, born 20 June 1840.

A long line of mango trees along the Mackay-Eungella Road, were planted in the 1880s that delineates the extent of the Branscombe plantation, about 1km east of Pleystowe Mill. The Marten family home, Winterbourne, was built on Branscombe Plantation, by Edward McKenzie Scott in 1872, who had come to Mackay to build the first Customs house. The house was built in what became known as the Queenslander style – an upper story inclusive of drawing-room, dining-room and bedrooms, opening onto a wide, open verandah, with servant's quarters beneath, while a separate building located away from the main building housed a kitchen and bathroom. Stables were located some distance away. As the Martens were among some of the early plantation owners of the district, they socialised with the Rawson family from The Hollow, the Davidsons of Alexandra Plantation and the Finch Hatton family.[313]

Marten was a well-brought up young English lady of her time who had learned the skills of a water-colourist and painted scenes both within and outside of Winterbourne and of northern Queensland.[314] These paintings provided a window into the lifestyle of early plantation owners lives and the ways they adapted to life in the

---

[313] 'Annie Pring Marten: Water-Colour Artist', 2000, Pioneer Valley Museum, Mirani, Queensland.
[314] Annie Pring Marten, 2006, 'Afternoon Scene on the Front Verandah at Winterbourne, Mackay', *Trove*, viewed 2/02/2024, https://trove.nla.gov.au/work/

tropics. The painting above, along with a series of water colours painted during a trip by steamer to newly established goldfield township of Cooktown, were sent home to family members in England.[315]

Another hobby of Marten was that of gardening. She transformed the wilderness surrounding Winterbourne into a formal English-style garden (using Australian fauna) with sweeping driveways overlooking the Pioneer River. A collection of photographs depicts her entertaining friends in the grounds of Winterbourne, including the Rawsons and the Finch Hattons who had known each other in England. Horse-riding was another pastime as were social engagements such as horse-races, balls and concerts.

Two children, Frank and Winifred, were born to the Martens while at Winterbourne: Frank Tucker, born 29 September 1873, died 6 January 1874. (He was buried at Branscombe); and Winifred, (born 12 December 1874-1963). They had three children when they returned to England: George Ernest (was born 1 February 1877-1940); Francis Arthur (was born 7 January 1879-1950); and Agnes Clara (born 26 August 1880-1940).[316]

The sugar industry was devastated by the disease 'rust' in the 1860s and 70s which impacted the Martens to the extent that George Marten went bankrupt, and the properties were sold up in 1876. At the same time, George Marten's uncle (George Robert Marten) died, and George was recalled to England to take charge of a family-owned bank.[317]

Marten then travelled with Winifred and a maid by ship to southern ports on the *Yaralla* to sail further onto England on 25 September 1876. The family returned to the Martens family residence at Marshals Wick, near St Albans, Hertfordshire, England. Marten

---

[315] Mackay Family History Society, 2012, 'Annie Pring Marten: Water-Colour Artist', Mackay, The Society.
[316] Wright, Bernice, [202?], Mackay, *Facebook*, Vintage Queensland.
[317] Mackay Family History Society, 2012, 'Annie Pring Marten', op. cit.

raised her children there following the sudden death of her husband on 25 August 1905 at Crowborough, and continued her role in community, church, education and scouting interests. She died 8 January 1933 at Rousham, Hall Place Gardens, St Albans, Hertfordshire, England.[318]

A collection of Annie Pring Marten's artwork and photograph albums of Mackay in the 1870s were presented to the Mackay Regional Council in 1968 by an English grandson. The paintings are now in the Artspace Collections and the photograph albums are in the Mackay Regional Council's Heritage Collection.

Events:
- 1872 Resided at Winterbourne
- 1876 Returned to England

Figure 41 Entrance to Pleystowe Station. Annie Marten 1873. Photograph courtesy of the Mackay Regional Council, Artspace Collection.

---

[318] ibid.

Martin, Elizabeth Watt (1846-1911)

Figure 42 Elizabeth Watt Martin. Photograph courtesy of the Queensland State Archives.

Born:
- 14 January 1846
- Edinburgh, Midlothian, Scotland

Died:
- 28 April 1911
- Mandarana, Mackay, Queensland

Occupation:
- Missionary and grazier - Martin donated land at her Mandarana property (Formerly spelt Mandurana) to begin a Pacific Islander mission in 1882. St. Peter's Church and a consecrated cemetery were established on Robinson's land in 1884. Her legacy is now an historical focus for the district.

Alternative Name/s:
- Elizabeth Watt Pringle, Elizabeth Martin.

Summary:

Elizabeth Watt Pringle was the daughter of Thomas Pringle and Elizabeth Waddell Martin. Her middle name of Watt came from her paternal grandmother, Elizabeth Watt Pringle. Martin was baptised at Saint Cuthberts, Edinburgh on 15 February 1846. She met Robert (Bob) Martin while he was on holiday in Scotland. Her marriage to Martin took place at the home of her brother at Saint Michael, Wood Green, Haringey near London on 1 January 1876. Robert was 35 and Elizabeth was aged 29. He was born to James and Eliza Martin at Leadhills, Lanarkshire, Scotland. The couple had five children at the Mandarana property who survived to adulthood and three who died at a young age. Those who became adults were Alice Rachel Martin Macdonnell (1877-1955), Rachel Majoribanks Martin (1880-1956), Robin William Martin (1883- 2001), Frank Martin (1890-1964) and Gilbert Martin (1888-1967),[319] who served in the First World War.[320]

In 1882, Martin established a mission for the Pacific Islanders on the family property at Mandarana which continued to operate for some time. She donated land for the building of a church. Peter Bolo was one Solomon Islander from Santa Isabel Island who kept the prayer book she gave him, and his confirmation card, until his death in old age.[321]

Martin and Reverend Albert McLaren had planned and designed St Peter's Church at Mandarana. They commenced fund raising to build the church and were assisted by Martin's friend, Helen (Nellie) Porter Mitchell who soon became Nellie Armstrong and then the world-famous diva, Dame Nellie Melba. Mitchell sang at a concert held in the old School of Arts, Wood Street, Mackay.[322] She also contributed to the repair of the church after cyclone Eline

---

[319] *Deaths in the District of Mackay in the Colony of Queensland*, 1898, 'Robert Martin', Queensland, Family History Research Service, viewed 15/08/2024 https://www.familyhistory.bdm.qld.gov.au/
[320] 'Frank Martin', 2024, Ancestry.com.au, viewed 19/08/2024, www.ancestry.com.au
[321] Mackay Family History Society, 2020, 'Mandarana Church and Cemetery', viewed 13/08/2024, https://www.mackayfamilyhistory.org.au/mandarana-church-and-cemetery...
[322] ibid.

and again for the re-building of St Peter's Church after the 1918 cyclone. Alice Martin wrote to Melba describing the damage to the church. Melba responded by sending a cheque for £20.[323]

St. Peter's Church was built by 1884. It was a wooden building that included hopper windows, a vestry and sanctuary. It was opened on 13 April 1884 during Easter by the Reverend T Worthington. The chalice and paten were a gift from the former Rector, Reverend Albert Maclaren. Following the two cyclones, Frank Martin stored the windows in a long pine case on a sheltered upstairs verandah until the church was rebuilt.

As a second-generation Martin, he carried the 1884 chalice and paten (in their special wooden box) to and from the church on horseback until the church closed. When funds were needed for the church, a dance was held at Coningsby School and The Leap Hall. St Peter's had a golden jubilee in 1934 which drew a large congregation. St Peter's closed in 1962, and on 5 August 1968 was accidently burnt down.[324]

Robert Martin died of chronic diarrhoea and pneumonia in 1898. He was buried under a blue gum tree on the edge of the cemetery about 30 feet from the church. The Mandarana Cemetery is the only church cemetery in Mackay. Two Pacific Islanders were also buried near the cemetery. The cemetery was declared sacrosanct by a third-generation owner of the Martin family who purchased the property in 1964 when Frank Martin (who had never married) died. It is understood forty-nine people were buried in the cemetery in thirty-four graves.[325]

The Mandarana Cemetery was subsequently donated to the Mackay Regional Council. Since then, an area of 2.5 acres, inclusive of the original church site, was privately purchased by a family who have contracted to maintain the cemetery. Elizabeth Martin died at the age of 65 and was buried in the Mackay City Cemetery.

---
[323] 'The Mandarana Church', 1920, *Daily Mercury*, Wednesday 21 January, p.6.
[324] Mackay Family History Society, 2020, op. cit.
[325] ibid.

Events:
- 1876 Arrived in Australia
- 1882 Anglican mission began
- 1884 St Peter's Church was first built
- 1968 St Peter's Church accidently burnt down

Links:

National Trust of Queensland, Mandarana Church and Cemetery 140th Anniversary. https://nationaltrustqld.org.au/whats-on/mandarana-church-cemetery-140th-anniversary

Mackay Regional Council, Pioneer Heritage Driving Trail https://www.mackay.qld.gov.au/__data/assets/pdf_file/0007/356722/Pioneer_Valley_Heritge_Driving_Trail_Brochure_web.pdf

Figure 43 Saint Peter's Church, Mandarana Cemetery, 2024. A scaled down version of the original Church façade lists the names of those in the cemetery.

Melba, Nellie (1861-1931) Dame GBE

Figure 44 Helen Porter Armstrong. Courtesy of *Find a Grave*.

Born:
- 19 May 1861
- 'Doonside', Richmond, Yarra City, Victoria, Australia.

Died:
- 23 February 1931
- Darlinghurst, Sydney, New South Wales.

Occupation:
- Melba was a prima donna, opera singer, soprano, mezzo soprano, lyric Coloratura soprano, classical musician, philanthropist, and Dame of the British Empire. Dame Nellie Melba, an Australian opera singer, made an enormouse contribution to the world of opera globally and to the local community of Marian where she spent a few brief years.

Alternative Name/s:
- Helen Porter Mitchell, Helen Porter Armstrong, Nellie, Melba.

Summary:

Dame Nellie Melba was born Helen Porter Mitchell to Scottish born parents, the eldest surviving child of David Mitchell, (a building contractor in Melbourne and property owner) and Isabella Ann Mitchell nee Dow. Her parents had ten children in total, four boys and six girls. She was later called 'Nellie' by her parents. Her father was also a music lover who had a bass voice of beautiful quality and played the fiddle skilfully.[326] Her mother, Isabella, was an artist and proficiently played several instruments including the harmonium and was Nellie's first teacher. 'Her earliest recollection of music was crawling under a piano when she was four years of age, to listen with wonder and delight to her mother's playing.'[327]

Mitchell learned to play the piano with the assistance of two aunts who were music teachers, at aged 5. She first sang at a school concert when she was aged 6. 'Her initial number was "Shells of Ocean" followed by as an encore, 'Coming thro' the Rye.'[328] She continued to sing throughout her childhood at similar functions. Later, at age 14, she learned to play the organ and took professional singing lessons at school. She became a boarder at Leigh School, Bridge Road, Richmond. Later she attended the Presbyterian Ladies College as a daygirl. Her music teacher was Mme Ellen Christian. 'Melba showed herself to be adept in elocution, accomplished at painting and in acquiring the social graces; in mathematics and English she was undistinguished.'[329] At 18 years of age, she studied voice with an Italian tenor, Pietro Cecchi whose guidance provided a solid base for her career.

Leaving school in 1880 coincided with the death of her mother and a younger sister. As a change of scenery, her father decided to

---

[326] 'Dame Nellie Melba: Queen of Song', 1931, *Huon Times*, Thursday 26 February, p.6 viewed 10/06/2024 http://nla.gov.au/nla.news-article136354081
[327] 'Dame Melba's Career', 1931, *Kalgoorlie Miner*, Tuesday 24 February, p.4, viewed 10/06/2024 http://nla.gov.au/nla.newsarticle95213716
[328] ibid.
[329] Davidson, Jim, 2006, *Australian Dictionary of Biography*, viewed 9/06/2024 https://adb.anu.edu.au/

take both her and her sister Annie to Marian, near Mackay, where he had purchased a sugar mill. This mill was the forerunner of the Marian Cooperative Mill. Her future husband, who she met in 1882, was Charles Nesbit Frederick Armstrong, the manager of her fathers' mill.[330] Captain Armstrong was the sixth son of a baronet Sir Archibald Armstrong of Kings County, now known as County Offaly. He was tall, blue-eyed, a skilled horseman and boxer and three years her senior. As a 21-year-old, Mitchell must have been impressed. On arrival in Australia, Armstrong became engaged in the sugar cane industry in the Marian district.[331]

The couple were married in Brisbane on 23 February 1931. They had a son George Nesbit Armstrong. A former resident remembers seeing Miss Nellie Mitchell when she lived on her father's property – a property which required three fords to be crossed in crocodile infested waters, just to visit the property 25 miles from Mackay. Then as Mrs Charlie Armstrong, she would ride side saddle with the baby on a pillow in front of her. The writer's opinion was that not many young women would tolerate the difficulties she had to overcome in her young married life.[332]

In later years, Melba described her experiences living 'in the bush' in North Queensland with her husband who managed a sugar cane mill; 'We had a little house with a galvanised tin roof, desolate and lonely, with no other companionship other than that of birds and especially – of the reptiles.'[333] Soon after they first arrived, it rained for six weeks. 'My piano was mildewed, my clothes were damp, the furniture fell to pieces, spiders, ticks and other obnoxious insects penetrated into the house – to say nothing

---

[330] 'Church Where Melba Sang', 1947, *Daily Mercury*, Saturday 27, p.9. viewed 9/06/2024 http://nla.gov.au/nla.news-article171163808
[331] 'Married in Mackay: Melba's Husband Dies', 1948, *Daily Mercury*, Friday 5 November, p.2., viewed 13/06/2024 http://nla.gov.au/nla.news-article171441889
[332] 'A Memory of Melba,1931', *Newcastle Morning Herald and Miner's' Advocate*, Saturday 28 February, p.8. viewed 20/06/2024 http://nla.gov.au/nla.news-article137687029
[333] 'Church Where Melba Sang', 1947, *Daily Mercury*, Saturday 27 September, p.9. viewed 13/06/2024 http://nla.gov.au/nla.news-article171163808

of snakes which had a habit of appearing underneath one's bed at the most inappropriate moments.'[334]

The house in which she lived during her brief marriage (known as Nightingale's Cottage or Retreat) was relocated from the old mill site to the banks of the Pioneer River at Marian and is now a tourist attraction housing Melba memorabilia and a café.[335]

Prior to becoming world famous, Mitchell taught two sons of the Rawson family to play the piano. She is quoted as saying in her autobiography, 'Had it not been for my two friends, Mr and Mrs Charles Rawson, I do not know what I should have done.'[336] Mitchell sang at many charitable events in the Mackay district. One event was at the Albion Hotel in Walkerston as Helen Porter 'Nellie' Mitchell in 1881. She also sang at a fund raiser for the South Sea Island Mission built on the Martin property at Mandarana, near The Leap, Mackay. This event on behalf of the mission, was a fund raiser concert held at the School of Arts, Wood Street, Mackay. As Helen Porter Armstrong, she was baptised in the Holy Trinity Church, Mackay before embarking on her career as Nellie Melba.[337]

Melba, named after her hometown of Melbourne (where her father had financial interests), sought a career in the south - mainly Melbourne and Sydney - but it was not the career she had in mind, so she set sail for England. The opportunity became available when her father, David Mitchell, was appointed Commissioner to the Indian and Colonial Exhibition held in London in 1856. Melba, her husband and her baby son George travelled with her father. His offer extended to payment of one year's lessons with her preferred teacher. After contacting London based trainers and refusals, she selected Madame Mathilde Marchesi in Paris.[338] Her

---

[334] ibid.
[335] Nellie Melba Museum, 2024, viewed 11/12/2024 https://nelliemelbamuseum.com.au/marian-queensland-homes-dame-nellie-melba-museum/
[336] 'Church Where Melba Sang', 1947, *Daily Mercury,* op. cit.
[337] Mackay Family History Society, 2020, 'Mandarana Church and Cemetery', viewed 17/06/2024 https://www.mackayfamilyhistory.org.au/mandarana-church-and-cemetery/
[338] 'Dame Melba's Career', 1931, *Kalgoorlie Miner,* Tuesday 24 February, p.4. viewed 20/06/2024 http://nla.gov.au/nla.news-article95213716

success and road to fame never faulted from that point in time. She became a world-renowned opera singer of the late Victorian era, the likes of which has not been equalled and the first Australian to achieve international recognition as a classical musician.[339]

The local community of Marian and the Mackay district celebrated the life of Melba by establishing Melba House, at Marian, a museum displaying photographs and memorabilia in the house where she had once lived with her husband that had been transported to the museum site on the bank of the Pioneer River at Marian. Dame Nellie Melba was featured on the $100 Australian bank note. Melba held so many 'final' concerts that the term, 'do a Melba' became an accepted term for repeat performances.[340]

> Two plaques in memory of Dame Nellie Melba were erected at Marian, 22 miles from Mackay. The president of the Queensland branch of the Royal Geographical Society of Australia performed the ceremony. The plaques have been erected on memorial gates at the mill and the house where Melba lived with Herbert Charles Armstrong in 1883[341] when Armstrong was manager of the old Balmoral Mill.[342]

Dame Nellie Melba was unique not only to Australia but to the world. Melba's voice was remarkable for its even quality over a range of nearly three octaves, and for its pure, silvery timbre. She had international renown as a soprano, performing in many cities including Milan, Brussels, London, Paris and New York.[343] She died in Sydney on 23 February 1931 and was buried in Lilydale Cemetery beside her father and mother.

---

[339] The Australian Women's Register, viewed 11/12/2024, https://www.womenaustralia.info/entries/melba-nellie/
[340] 'Melba's Career', 1931, *Moree Gwydir Examiner and General Advertiser*, Thursday 26, p.5. viewed 3/06/2023 http://nla.gov.au/nla.news-article111694955
[341] '*The Courier Mail*, 1951, May 7, viewed 29/06/2024 https://www.monumentaustralia.org.au/themes/people/arts/display/104402-dame-nellie-melba
[342] 'Church Where Melba Sang', op. cit.,
[343] Reserve Bank of Australia', 2024, Dame Nellie Melba, viewed 29/06/2024 https://banknotes.rba.gov.au/australias-banknotes/people-on-the-banknotes/dame-nellie-melba/

Events:

- 1875-1880; Melba's early education was in Melbourne
- 1881; Following the death of her mother and sister, Melba travelled to Mackay, Queensland, with her father where he purchased a sugar mill.
- 1884; Melba returned to Melbourne to begin a professional singing career and gave several concerts and recitals.
- 1886; Melba accompanied her father to London and chose her professional name as Melba, an abbreviation of her hometown, Melbourne.
- 1902; Melba's triumphant homecoming involved a concert tour of all Australian states and New Zealand.
- 1903; Melba returned to Europe in 1903 but came back to Australia many times.
- 1904–1926; During this time Melba made almost two-hundred recordings.
- 1909; She toured the Australian outback. In the same year, she bought a property at Coldstream near Lilydale, Victoria and employed the architect John Grainger (father of the composer Percy Grainger) to design Coombe Cottage.
- 1911, 1924, 1928; During these years Melba brought the Melba-Williamson Opera Company to Australia.
- 1914–1918; Based in Australia during World War I, Melba worked tirelessly to raise funds for war charities. She also gave wartime concerts in North America. For her services to the war effort, Melba was made a Dame Commander of the Order of the British Empire in 1918. During this period, she established a singing school at the Melbourne Conservatorium of Music in Albert Street, later renamed the Melba Memorial Conservatorium of Music, providing her services free of charge. She often travelled from Lilydale to teach her 'Melba's Girls'.
- 1920; She became the first artist of international standing to participate in direct radio broadcasts.
- 1926; Melba gave several supposedly 'final' performances. Her final Covent Garden performance was in 1926.

- 1927; She sang at the opening of Parliament House in Canberra and was made a Dame Grand Cross of the Order of the British Empire.
- 1928; Her final and emotional concerts took place in Australia.
- 1931; Melba died in Sydney on 23 February 1931 and was buried at the Lilydale Cemetery in Victoria.
- 2008; The private conservatorium, Melba Memorial Conservatorium of Music, ceased teaching and became the Dame Nellie Melba Opera Trust.[344]

Links:

Davidson, Jim, 1986, Dame Nellie Melba (1861-1931), Australian Dictionary Biography, viewed 2/04/2023 https://adb.anu.edu.au/biography/melba-dame-nellie-7551

Dame Nellie Melba Museum, 2024, viewed 20/03/2024 https://nelliemelbamuseum.com.au/brief-biography-dame-nellie-melba-museum/

Figure 45 Dame Nellie Melba. Photograph courtesy of the Melba Opera Trust.

---

[344] ibid.

Neilsen, Beryl Anne OAM (1941-2023)

Figure 46 Beryl Neilsen OAM. Photograph courtesy of Australian of the Year Awards, 2022.

Born:
- 30 November 1941
- Mackay, Queensland.

Died:
- 3 July 2023
- Mackay, Queensland.

Occupation:
- Grazier and philanthropist. Neilsen was Isaac Regional Council's Citizen of the Year in 2018 and awarded the Order of Australia Medal (OAM) in 2022.

Alternative Name/s:
- Beryl Nielsen, Beryl Smith

Summary:

Beryl was the daughter of Mary Cecelia Ryalls and James Wilfred Smith of Mackay. She had two brothers Ron and John Smith. The Smith children attended school at St Francis Xavier Catholic Primary School and then onto secondary school at St Patrick's College, Mackay. Smith was a Mackay girl who worked for a company that flew supplies to central Queensland properties when she met a man sent from a station to collect an engine part. This man was John Oliver Neilsen whom she married on 5 May 1962 at St Francis Xavier Church, West Mackay. They lived on Olive Downs Station from 1962 until 1980 when they moved to Winchester Downs Station from 1980 until she relocated to Mackay in 2020. She continued to visit Winchester Downs with the aid of family and friends. The couple were childless. Neilsen lost her husband John in May of 1989 when he was 46 years old.

Winchester Downs was a family-run cattle property about 30 km south of Moranbah, in the Bowen Basin mining area. Three mining companies encroach on the grazing property. These were Peak Downs, Millennium and Eagle Downs. The size of the grazing property had reduced over time.[345] Davy quoting Neilsen, 'It was very sad at first. There were lots of tears in the beginning, she said. But it's called progress, and we learnt to accept it would happen'.[346]

As a widow, Neilsen sold a large part of her stake in the property Winchester Downs, with the intention of bequeathing her estate but was advised to spend the money helping others. Neilsen took that advice and established the John & Beryl Neilsen Winchester Foundation in 2011 to support the education of rural and remote Queensland students, a dream long held by her and her husband.

The Foundation, which helps families cover the costs of boarding school and university, aims to give country children the same

---

[345] Davy, Andrea, 2014, "Helping to Build Bush', *Rural Weekly: Central Queensland Edition*, October 3, p.1.
[346] ibid.

opportunities as those from the city. It has as its ethos to *'Create Education Opportunities for Country Children'*. 'I didn't have children, and my husband died quite a while ago now, so I have a real purpose in life now she said.'[347]

Neilsen enjoyed being with children. 'When I am with children, you can't wipe the smile off my face', she said.[348] Children would write her letters all the time. Some of the graduates included several veterinarians, an electrical engineer, and a surgeon. 'Kids need their education. So many have gone through now and they've turned out marvellously', Neilsen said.[349] As of 2012 when the first scholarships were awarded, there have been 387 scholarships given out. Beryl Neilsen said there was a great need for access to education in rural Queensland, particularly those families on properties who home school their children. It can be isolated in rural areas.[350]

From 2013, the Winchester Foundation commenced the primary school students annual Whitsunday Voices Youth Literature Festival, held at the Whitsunday Anglican School's campus in Mackay. The festival accepts students from rural and remote areas including the Brigalow Schools, Pioneer Valley Schools, Country School north and south of Mackay as well as students from Capricornia School of Distance Education Rockhampton and Charters Towers School of Distance Education Outreach Group. The Foundation covers the cost of admission to the festival, accommodation, food and transport for over 3,200 students. Each student is gifted a Winchester shirt.[351] Neilsen also hosted a 'Winchester Day', on her property, where recipients

---

[347] Gunders, Jody, 2017, 'Winchester Foundation Scholarships for Remote Youth Bearing Fruit for Queensland philanthropist', *ABC Rural*, 14 June, viewed 20/05/2024 https://www.abc.net.au/rural/2017-06-14/winchester-foundation..
[348] ibid.
[349] ibid.
[350] ibid.
[351] Macrossan and Amiet Solicitors, 2021, 'Beryl Neilsen OAM', viewed 20/04/2024 https://cms.australianoftheyear.org.au/recipients/beryl-neilsen-oam

and their families were invited to a luncheon that offers them an opportunity to thank their host and her team in person and for families to connect.

The Foundation has also been the main sponsor for the Isolated Children's and Parent's Association Conference (ICPA) since 2014. A representative of ICPA described being 'thrilled' to learn the Neilsen had been awarded an OAM. 'ICPA Queensland is thrilled to hear that Beryl has received an OAM', Ms Martin said. "Beryl has been a wonderful advocate for rural and remote students and has enabled many students to access education through her generous sponshorship.'[352]

Neilsen was named Issac Regional Council's Citizen of the Year in 2018.[353] Beryl Neilsen was awarded the Order of Australia Medal for service to the community through her charitable organisation, namely the John & Beryl Neilsen Winchester Foundation. The award was presented at a ceremony held at Government House, Brisbane on 21 September 2021. Neilsen was also a nominee for the Senior Australian of the Year in 2022.[354] Beryl Neilsen died at the age of 82 and was buried at Walkerston Cemetery beside her husband John.

Events:

- *1962* Olive Downs Station.
- 1980 Winchester Downs Station.
- 2011 John & Beryl Neilsen Winchester Foundation.
- 2013 Founded the Whitsunday Voices Youth Literature Festival.

---

[352] Whiting, Melanie, 2021, 'Moranbah Grazier and Philanthropist Beryl Neilsen Awarded the OAM', *Daily Mercury*, June 13, viewed 20/04/2024 https://www.couriermail.com.au/news/queensland/mackay/moranbah-grazier-and-philanthropist-beryl-neilsen-awarded-oam-news-story/e743770561f29b788796ba195e35f44d

[353] ibid.

[354] 'Beryl Neilsen OAM: Founder and Director of the Winchester Foundation', 2022, viewed 17/05/2024 https://cms.australianoftheyear.org.au/receipents/beryl-neilsen-oam

- 2014 Main sponsor Isolated Children's and Parent's Association Conference since 2014.
- 2018 Issac Regional Council's Citizen of the Year.
- 2021 Order of Australia Medal (OAM).
- 2022 Nominee for Senior Australian of the Year.

Links:

Winchester Foundation: https://winchesterfoundation.org/

Figure 47 Beryl Neilsen. Photograph courtesy of the John & Beryl Neilsen Winchester Foundation.

Ramsamy, Nolear (1917-2021)

Figure 48 Nolear Ramsamy as a young woman published in 2013. Photograph published in 2013 courtesy of the *Courier-Mail*.

Born:
- 6 October 1917
- Port Liu, Prince of Wales Island, Torres Shire, Queensland, Australia

Died:
- 22 March 2021
- Slade Point, Mackay, Queensland

Occupation:
- Elder, Torres Strait Island community and centenarian.

Alternative Name/s:
- Nolia (Nolear) Syed Bin Baba, Nolear Barba and Nana Ramsamy

Summary:

Nolear Baba, was the fourth child born of thirteen children to Siat (Syed) Marmin Bin Baba (of Malaysian descent) and Mariam Moy. She was born at Port Liu on Prince of Wales Island, Torres Strait. Her father, Siat was from Malacca and at 17 years of age, travelled to Thursday Island where he met Mariam who was born on Badu Island.[355] This was in the late 1800s to early 1900s when Australia's population was around 5 million people.

As a young woman, she enjoyed Island life. She fished and hunted with her brothers and went to the picture show with her sisters. Her young life was full of fun and mischief but always working hard to support the growing family. She cleaned and worked with her father, cutting firewood and working on the pearl farms. She obtained money to watch films by using a broom stick to knock rats from the rafters for which she was paid a bounty. She became an expert rat catcher, but the downside was the holes that were left in the roof of their home. Her eldest daughter Rhonda was born in 1936, followed by Nami in 1938.[356]

The family was evacuated, along with many of the Thursday Island population in 1942 to Cherbourg in North Queensland following the declaration of war between Australia and Japan. It was in 1942 that George VI was King, John Curtin was Prime Minister, and the population of Australia numbered around seven million.[357]

Baba was a 24-year-old mother of two children (Rhonda and Nami) and pregnant with Salma. The journey took them by ship and barge from Thursday Island to Townsville then by truck to Cherbourg. Other family groups who were also evacuated with them; the Ahmats and Ahwangs amongst others.

---

[355] *Facebook*, 2017, 'Nolear Ramsamy', viewed 20/12/2023 https://www.facebook.com/search/top/?q=Nolear%20Ramsamy
[356] ibid.
[357] ibid.

Whilst in Cherbourg, the family lived on rations issued by the government. The sisters would walk 7 km to Murgon to get supplies so that everyone could eat. She made friends with the local Aboriginal community. Aunty Rita Huggins became one of her best friends. Salma was born at Cherbourg in 1942. The family left Cherbourg in 1943 settling in Mackay. Nan's mother, father and four siblings, as well as her three young children lived in the three-bedroom house on Harbour Road, North Mackay. It must have been a very busy house.[358]

To support the family, Baba worked several jobs as a cleaner, laundry hand and ticket seller at the local show. Whilst working at the show, she met a handsome showman of Indian descent from Lawrence in NSW, Edward Royce Ramsamy – known as Ram Chandra.[359]

Nolear and Edward Royce Ramsamy BEM OAM (Ram Chandra 1921-1998) were married in 1944 at the Mackay Court House which was followed by a reception at the family home in North Mackay.[360] The newlyweds soon moved to Thornber Street North Mackay. Nan's father, Siat died in 1945 in Brisbane whilst working away from home. After Siat's passing, Mariam, his wife, moved back to the Thursday Island, where she lived until she died.

Over the following years, the Ramsamy family grew to twelve children -six girls and five boys. Joining Rhonda; Nami and Salma are Edward Royce Jnr in 1945; Albert in 1947; John Mirman in 1948; Nolear (Sissy) in 1949; Annette in 1951; Brian in 1952; Lawrence in 1954; and Maree in 1956. One baby was born and died

---

[358] ibid.
[359] Hudson, Fallon, 2009, 'Tribute to Snake Man Ram Chandra', *The Courier Mail*, June 19 viewed 3/10/2023, https://www.couriermail.com.au/news/queensland/mackay/tribute-to-snake-man-ram-chandra/news-story/e68ffc0b411a1f8cac7b33b3125eeb42
[360] Barba, Nolear, 1944, 'Marriage Registration', Queensland Government, Brisbane, The Government, 29 November, viewed 11/12/2023 https://familyhistorty.bdm.qld.gov.au

on 6 October 1958.³⁶¹ The first grandchild, Gail was born in 1956 to Nami and in 1958 the whole family moved to Slade Point.³⁶²

Over the next forty years, the Wren Street property would become not only the local for family Christmas gatherings, but Ramsamy had created a menagerie of animals which included snakes, chickens, goats, sheep, aviaries of birds, cockatoos and ponds for fish.

Whilst her husband travelled the countryside educating people about the Taipan and snake bites, Nolear, with support from her elder children, took care of her large family. Although, at times life was hard, she had strong faith and the family came first. She would make sure that any new suitor or potential in-law was able to provide for the family. She made them go into the mangroves to collect shellfish or pick oysters and penny winkles from the rocks. This became a rite of passage.

As a Torres Strait Islander family, living off the ocean and mangroves and hunting and fishing were always considered important, not only as a source of food for the family but also as a celebration of culture. Cultural celebrations would also be marked by a huge gathering of family members preparing vermicelli and curry chicken and traditional Island food, dancing and laughter. Ramsamy had a sense of fun and was not to be left out of activities with her children and grandchildren.

When her grandsons would go crocodile hunting, Ramsamy, then in her 70s, would be first in the boat, holding the spotlight and directing her sons where to go. She would be the loudest barracker on the sideline at football matches when her grandchildren were playing. During State of origin, Ram, the New South Welshman, would be barracking for the Maroons whilst she would stir the pot by cheering on the Blues.³⁶³

---

[361] Ramsamy, Nolear Barba, 2021, *Find A Grave*, viewed 10/02/2023, https://www.findagrave.com/memorial/227144386/nolear-ramsamy

[362] Ramsamy, Nolear, 1972, *Australian Electoral Commission*, viewed 12/03/2023 https://www.ancestry.com.au

[363] Ramsamy, Nolear, 2022, *Facebook* comments by friends and family.

Ramsamy was always willing to travel back to the Torres Strait whenever possible and to other far-flung places such as Melbourne, Darwin, Canberra, Cairns and Newcastle, to see her growing and extended family. A shopping trip to town with Ramsamy would take twice as long as planned as she would meet so many people who would come up to her to say hello. Only a few weeks before her death, she was out fishing with grandson Michael and his wife at Grasstree; - still trying to out fish him.[364]

There were always fun times with tears of laughter flowing whenever she met with her sisters and brothers, retelling stories of their lives together. Her husband Ram Chandra died in 1998 and Ramsamy remained in the big house at Slade Point which she shared with him surrounded by photographs and memories of her family. During her first 100 years she had seen four British Monarchs, twenty-five prime Ministers and the Australian population grow from 5 million to 24.7 million. At her 100th birthday celebration, the 197 (known) family members were represented by: twelve children, thirty-nine grandchildren, ninety-seven great-grandchildren, forty-seven great-great-grandchildren and three great-great-great-grandchildren.[365] Ramsamy died on 22 March 2021 and was buried at Mount Bassett Cemetery with her husband Edward Royce Ramsamy.

Events:

- 1942 Moved from Prince of Wales Island, Torres Strait to Cherbourg, Queensland.
- 1943 Moved with family to North Mackay.
- 1958 Moved to Wren Street in Slade Point, Mackay.
- 2017 Held 100 birthday celebrations.

---

[364] *Facebook*, 2017, '100 birthday celebrations with family and friends.
[365] Summary based on speech given at Norlear Ramsamy's 100th birthday celebrations, published on *Facebook*, viewed 2023-01-23 https://www.*facebook*.com/profile.php?id=100063575708966

Links:

Petith, Heidi, 2021, 'Nolear Ramsamy: Community Mourns Death of Nanna, a Matriarch of Mackay Indigenous Community,' *Daily Mercury*, viewed 20/07/2024 https://www.couriermail.com.au/news/queensland/mackay/nolear-ramsamy-community-mourns-death-of-nanna-a-patriarch-of-mackay-Indigenous-family/news-story/c8e820382d172f7b9afe823a0672de5a

Loveday, Ashalea, 2021, Celebrating the Life of Nolear Ramsamy: Nolear Ramsamy Tribute, Mackay Regional Council (MECC) viewed 20/07/2024 https://www.youtube.com/watch?v=XV1rUUeHCN8

Figure 49 Nolear Ramsamy aged 100 in 2017.
Photograph courtesy of *Facebook*.

Ready, Mary (1832-1902)

Figure 50 Mary Ready. Photograph courtesy of Mackay Family History Society.

Born:
- About 1832
- Cappagh White, County Tipperary, Ireland

Died:
- 6 April 1902
- Mackay, Queensland, Australia

Occupation:
- Ready, a hotelier, was reportedly the first European woman to arrive in the Mackay district. Ready's daughter was believed to be the first European child born in the Mackay district and Ready was associated with the myth surrounding 'The Woman at the Leap'.

Alternative Name/s:
- Mary Hayes

Summary:

Mary Ready, formerly Hayes, has the distinction of being the first Northern European woman to live in the Mackay district. Hayes was born in the village of Cappagh White, Tipperary in about 1832. At the age of 21, following the death of her parents, Charles Hayes and Mary (nee Dwyer), Hayes travelled to Australia on the New Zealand sailing ship, *Matoaka*, arriving in Sydney on 17 March 1855. This ship was later lost at sea in 1869.[366] She married James Ready, an Irishman from Lornell, Limerick, Ireland, in Sydney, NSW, on 10 April 1858. They had four children, Charles Patrick, Catherine Agnes, James Joseph and Mary Josephine.

The couple worked on Gordonbrook Station, now situated near Grafton on the Clarence River, where their first child Charles was born at Gordon, NSW, in 1861. They travelled by bullock wagon to Fassifern Station in Queensland where Richard Spencer was forming a party to take a mob of cattle to the headquarters of the Denison Creek. James oversaw the bullock wagons and Mary cooked for the men. After the mammoth task of guiding the wagons and cattle across the Connors Range, the party rested at Connors River.[367]

It was here that Ready gave birth under the bullock wagon to her second child, a daughter, Catherine (Kate) in 1862. Kate was reported to have been the first European child born in Mackay district. Charles accompanied his parents on the long trip overland by bullock wagon to Mackay arriving in early 1862, before Mackay had been named. He became a prominent local businessman and later Mayor of Mackay (1903-1913).[368]

Spencer's party founded The Retreat Station (later Mt. Spencer Station). The Ready's then worked on Government Station where

---

[366] Wikitree, 2023, *Matoaka*, viewed 14/03/2023, https://www.wikitree.com/wiki/Space:Ship_Matoaka
[367] Mackay Family History Society, 2012, 'Mary Ready', Mackay, The Society.
[368] 'Mackay Mayors: Charles Patrick Ready 1903, 1913' viewed 28-1-2025 https://www.mackayhistory.org

their third child James was born in 1866. Captain John Mackay wrote, 'Mary Ready was the first white woman north of the Broadsound Range, and many of the old fever-stricken pioneers, since scattered far and wide, must, to the last, retain grateful memories of her kind attentions while presiding at Spencer's Camp.'[369]

The Readys purchased the newly built Travellers Rest Hotel at Hazledean (later the Range Hotel) near Eton Range, which they managed for many years.[370] Their fourth child, Mary, was born there in 1872. It was also while living there that the Leap incident occurred. It was reported and what has now become a widely debated legend, that in 1867, following an altercation in Cremorne and other districts, an Aboriginal woman jumped with a baby girl (who was wrapped in a stolen shawl), from the peak of Mt Mandarana (formerly Mt Johansburg) near what is now The Leap Hotel, about 21 km from Mackay.[371]

The baby girl was reportedly rescued by James Ready. The incident of a woman who was chased by Native Mounted Police to her death by jumping off the cliff, may have been a separate one to the adoption and rearing of an Aboriginal female child – two to three years old. The Ready family was said to have reared this girl. They had the girl christened Joanna (although she was known as Judy). She later used the surname of Hazledene, the district from where she came. The Ready's later owned Fort Cooper Station, properties at Baker's Creek, at Racecourse and in Mackay.[372]

---

[369] Hall, Glen, 2017, 'Mackay Mayors Charles Patrick Ready 1903, 1913', *Mackay History,* Mackay viewed 13/03/2023 http://mackayhistory.org/research/mayors/026_ready_cp.html

[370] Hall, Glenn, 2004, 'Mackay Cemeteries: Hazledean (Eton Range) Cemetery', viewed 10/04/2023 http://www.mackayhistory.org/research/cemeteries/hazledean_cemetery.html

[371] Moore, Clive, 1990, 'Blackgin's Leap: A Window into Aboriginal-European Relations in the Pioneer Valley, Queensland in the 1860s', pp 61-79, In, *Mackay Mercury and South Kennedy Advertiser* April 24, 1867, p 2 http://nla.gov.au/nla.news-article169701076.

[372] McDonald, Carmel and Dawn Bilney, 2013, 'James and Mary Ready', Mackay Family History, Society, viewed 17/03/2023 https://www.mackayfamilyhistory.org.au/james-and-mary-ready

There were many times when Mary Ready had to manage her children alone when her husband was absent. However, she never lost her pioneering spirit and compassion for others. She died in Mackay on 6 April 1902 and is buried in the Mackay Cemetery with her husband James.

Events:

- 1855 Arrived in Sydney, Australia.
- 1862 Arrived in Mackay district.
- 1864 Managed the Traveller's rest Hotel licensed in 1864.
- 1867 Baptism of Joanna (Judy) and Mary.

Links:

Mackay Cemeteries: Hazledean (Eton Range) Cemetery: http://www.mackayhistory.org/research/cemeteries/hazledean_cemetery.html

Women's Museum of Australia: https://wmoa.com.au/herstory-archive/ready-mary-hayes

Ehive: https://ehive.com/collections/3492/objects/77640/mrs-mary-ready-b-1834-cappawhite-tipperary-ireland-d-6th-april-1902-mackay-qld

The Range Hotel

Figure 51 The Range Hotel built by James Ready in 1864, was situated at Hazledean and destroyed by fire in 1990. Photograph courtesy of Mackay Historical Society.

Robinson, Mary Alexander Goodwin (1850-1925)

Figure 52 Mrs Robinson, Jack Talafuila and Sarah. Photograph courtesy of The Corporation of the Synod of the Diocese of North Queensland.

Born:
- 29 March 1850
- Agra, India

Died:
- 16 December 1925
- Paddington, London

Occupation:
- Missionary and educator of the indentured Pacific Islander sugar plantation workers located at Racecourse.[373]

Alternative Name/s:
- Mary Alexander Shaw

Summary:

Mary Alexander Shaw was born in India to Major William Alexander Shaw and Mary Grey, the fourth of six daughters.[374] She

---

[373] Mackay Family History Society, 2012, 'Mary Alexander Goodwin Robinson', Mackay, The Society.

[374] *England Census*, 1861, viewed 03/08/2024 https://www.ancestry.com.au

married Henry John Goodwin Robinson (a Lieutenant in the 98th regiment) on 15th of June 1869 in Guildford, Surrey, England. He was born in October of 1843, the son of Major John Robinson and Elizabeth Russell. Their first son of five children, Henry Alexander Robinson was born in Fort William, Hasting West Bengal, India, on 9 April 1970 and died on 19 April 1870 in West Bengal, India. Their second son Herbert Alexander Robinson was born on 26 of July 1871 in Guildford, Surrey, England. According to family history records, Emily Eleanor Stuart Robinson was baptised on 14 April 1873. At age 22 Mary Robinson sailed from London to Australia aboard the ship *Martaban* on 27 May 1873, with her husband and two children. Herbert was aged 2 years and Emily was aged 11 months. They arrived in Brisbane on 8 September 1873. Kathleen Grey Robinson were born on 6 February 1875[375] at Mackay and baptised at the Holy Trinity Church.

Henry Robinson and his two brothers had investments in dairying at Lorne around 1886. This business was transferred to Arthur Robinson in 1871 when the business became insolvent. Henry then became interested in the sugar industry and was appointed manager of Branscombe Mill in 1887. The mill was on the southside of the Pioneer River in the Parish of Greenmount.[376]

Reverend Albert Alexander McLaren, a missionary trained in England, was ordained and appointed to the 'difficult' parish of Mackay in 1878 through to 1883. He established a building fund in his first year, paid off Church debts and raised £1700 to build a new church. He supervised the new building (Holy Trinity Church) which opened in 1879. McLaren was appalled by the lack of education offered to Aboriginal people and Pacific Islanders. His powers of persuasion convinced Robinson to take on the task of a mission which commenced in 1882.[377]

---

[375] 'Henry John Goodwin Robinson Family Tree', viewed 20 June 2024 http://www.ancestry.com.au/
[376] Mackay Family History Society, 2012, 'Mary Alexander Goodwin Robinson', op. cit.
[377] Ford, Lyall, 2023, 'The Story of 'Heroic' Mackay Priest Albert Alexander McLaren', *The Courier Mail*, March 9, viewed 05/08/2024 https://www.couriermail.com.au

With colonialism of Queensland came Christianity, a mechanism of control in the British Solomon Islands Protectorate. The Islanders were susceptible to European influences when they were cut off from home and relatives. They responded to the interest and care shown to them by a few white religious people. One of those Mackay people taking an interest in the Islanders was Mary Robinson who established the Selwyn Mission, and another was Elizabeth Watt Martin at Mandarana plantation (formerly Mandurana), within the Church of England Pioneer Parish. The Selwyn Mission was named after Bishop Selwyn, who was the original organiser of the mission which belonged to the Church of England in the South Sea Islands.[378]

Robinson began the Selwyn Mission at the Te Kowai Plantation in 1882 at a site opposite Racecourse Mill.[379] The classes were initially conducted in her home and then moved to land donated by Meadowlands Plantation closer to Mackay before moving to Marian where Henry Robinson was Te Kowai Mill manager in 1884 and 1889 and the school was named 'Selwyn Mission.'[380]

In an 1890s report on the mission, it was noted that Robinson allowed the Islanders to wander through her home as if it was their own. She had always allowed this and said they had never abused the privilege. 'She is not only pastor and instructor, but doctor and sick nurse to the boys, and her house is her hospital. While there we saw one of her patients, a sick boy of 18, lying in a little room adjoining her house.' [381]

---

[378] 'Bishop Selwyn of the Melanesian Mission and the Labour Trade', 1885, *Brisbane Courier*, Friday 9 July, p.5., viewed 7/-8/2024 http://nla.gov.au/nla.news-article3437970
[379] *Selwyn House, Mackay*, 2007, Mackay Regional Council, viewed 31/08/2024 https://onesearch.slq.qld.gov.au/discovery/fulldisplay?context=L&vid=61SLQ_INST:SLQ&search_scope=Everything&tab=All&docid=alma99183695694102061
[380] Mackay Family History Society, 2012, 'Mary Alexander Goodwin Robinson', op. cit.
[381] Moore, Clive, 2017, *Making Mala: Malaita in Solomon Islands 1870s-1930s*, Canberra, ANU Press, p.153.

When visiting the Selwyn Mission at Marian on behalf of the Melanesian Mission in 1894, Reverend Brittain described the mission as 'worked on her own system', had 'gradually evolved' and was 'undoubtedly the best school in Queensland.'[382] Instruction was given in Pijin English which she regarded as better medium than English, and she worked 'single handed, and without any intermission as a rule even for an evening from year to year, and without any fund from which to supply the ordinary school materials.'[383] She taught reading, writing and arithmetic and prepared men for baptism and confirmation. Men walked from 9 to 20 km every evening to school, possibly without an evening meal, through the cold nights of July with seventy to eighty men in attendance.[384]

The form of the Ten Commandments they recited as described in the *North Queensland Jubilee Book* is as follows:

1. Man have 'em God one fellow, no have 'em 'nother fellow God
2. Man like God first time, everything behind
3. Man no swear
4. Man keep Sunday very good, day belong Big Master
5. Man very good 'long father and mother belong him
6. Man no kill
7. Man no take "Mary belong 'nother fellow man
8. Man no steal
9. Man no lie 'long 'nother fellow man
10. Man see good fellow something belong 'nother fellow man, he no want 'em all the time [385]

Robinson's work was undertaken in difficult circumstances. These were men who had been kidnapped or 'black-birded'

---

[382] ibid.
[383] ibid.
[384] ibid.
[385] *North Queensland Jubilee Book*, 1929, The Corporation of the Synod of the Diocese of North Queensland, Townsville, The Corporation, p.65.

from their homes and transported against their will for many years, nevertheless, they responded to the kindness shown by Robinson. She incurred the enmity of some Islanders by persuading them to give up their tribal feuds and give their weapons to her, resulting in threats to her life. On hearing this, some of the Malayta men who worked nearby, inscribed mystic signs on Robinson's gate indicating any harm coming to Robinson would result in the perpetrator's death by painful means. This was an effective form of protection for their instructor.[386] Many of Robinson's pupils went back to the Solomon Island and to New Guinea as lay preachers. One such man Dick Fohohlie, wrote:

> I never forget you. I pray every day and night for you. All our own boys we are, and all trying to do good work for God in New Guinea. We have been put to teach here so quickly because you been teach us fellows so much in Queensland. I think you were the best teacher in all Queensland. …God bless you always for ever and ever.[387]

Praise for her work came, not only from her pupils but also from the farmers, clergy and Bishops of the Anglican Church.[388] A Bishop described the Mackay school as being very successful. He said, pupils have left the Selwyn Mission and became missionaries in their home countries. He described her work as 'deserving of the highest recognition.'[389]

Branches of the mission were established on plantations and farms throughout the Pioneer Valley; at Te Kowai, Palms, Marian, Nindaroo, Meadowlands, Pioneer, Mandurama and The Leap.

---

[386] ibid.
[387] Wetherell, David, 1989, 'The Bridegroom Cometh: The Lives and Deaths of Queensland Melanesians in New Guinea 1893-1956', *Pacific Studies*, v.12, no.3, July, p.77.
[388] Crossman, WD, 1992, 'A Ticket to Heaven: The Selwyn Mission Mackay 1882-1904', rev. ed., [Mackay, Queensland, The Author.]
[389] 'Kanaka Mission at Mackay', 1894, *Brisbane Courier*, Monday 11 June, p.2. viewed 9/08/2024, http://nla.gov.au/nla.news-article3581447

One of Robinson's pupils, Luke Lowome, or Luke Logomier[390] (as Clive Moore writes) administered to Islanders at St Mary's Anglican Church at Farleigh until his death from influenza in 1919.[391]

In the mid-1890s, the mission returned to Meadowlands to where the Selwyn House was built on the donated land. Robinson continued to operate the mission under straitened circumstances. Due to a shortage of funds from the Bishop, Robinson considered closing the mission but instead a 'Robinson Fund' was established with £109 collected up until 1897 to subsidise her work.[392] In 1903, suffering poor health, Robinson left the district to retire to Adelaide and then onto England. The Anglican Synod took up a collection for Robinson and sent it to her. Henry John Goodwin Robinson died on 9 April 1916 at Guildford in Surrey and Mary Alexander Goodwin Robinson died in December 1925 at Paddington in London.[393] Selwyn House is a lasting visual memory of Mary Robinson, although it is not open to the public.

Events:

- 1882 Mary Goodwin Robinson opened bible classes for Melanesians which expanded into the Church of England Selwyn Mission
- 1882-1903 Established and managed the Selwyn Mission
- 1898 13 April at Holy Trinity parish, Mackay, Mary Goodwin Robinson was duly licenced as a Melanesian Teacher at the Selwyn Mission in the parish of the Holy Trinity, Mackay
- 1898 22 November, Mary Goodwin Robinson was licenced to perform the office of Missionary Teacher

---

[390] Moore, Clive, 2020, *Solomon Islands Historical Encyclopedia 1893-1978*, viewed 9/08/2024, https://www.solomonencyclopaedia.net/objects/D00000274...
[391] *North Queensland Jubilee Book*, op. cit., p.65.
[392] Moore, Clive, op. cit., p.165.
[393] Mackay Family History Society, 2012, 'Mary Alexander Goodwin Robinson', op. cit.

at the Selwyn Mission in the parish of Holy Trinity Mackay[394]
- 1903 Moved to Adelaide and subsequently returned to England

Links:

Mackay Regional Council Pioneer Valley Heritage Driving Trail https://www.mackay.qld.gov.au/__data/assets/pdf_file/0007/356722/Pioneer_Valley_Heritge_Driving_Trail_Brochure_web.pdf

Queensland Government Selwyn House https://apps.des.qld.gov.au/heritage-register/detail/?id=601080

Figure 53 Selwyn House 2000. Photograph courtesy of the State of Queensland, Queensland Heritage Register.

---

[394] 'Have You Seen the Old Mackay', 2015, *Facebook*, visited 2/03/2023 https://www.*facebook*.com/haveyouseentheoldmackay/photos/a.10155262157895034/10155014379825034/?type=3

Sam, Mary Ann (1866-1936)

Figure 54 Mary Ann Sam. Photograph courtesy of Glen Hall, Mackay Historical Society.

Born:
- 15 June 1866
- City of Cambridge, Cambridgeshire, England

Died:
- 26 0ctober 1936
- Hillcrest Rockhampton Private Hospital, Queensland.

Occupation:
- Community worker from Northside, Mackay.

Alternative Name/s:
- Mary Ann Sampson

Summary:

Mary Ann was the second youngest child of Joseph Sampson and Mary Ann Love. She arrived alone at Rockhampton (Keppel Bay) aboard the vessel *Northern Monarch* on 4 of March 1884 aged 17, as a domestic servant. Sampson met James Jung Sam (a farmer) who was twelve years her senior. He arrived in Mackay around 1877 at about the age of 23. He was born on Hong Kong Island, Hong Kong in June of 1854.[395] Choosing a partner of Chinese heritage in North Queensland was not unusual between 1847 and 1920 for Northern European woman, as compared to a male from a European background. Chinese men were known as hard workers, and they provided a regular income for their families, whereas European males were known to be fond of alcohol and often violent. Most of the marriages made by these couples were legal unions as it was in the best interest of the men to take advantage of the benefits offered as married men by the Colonial and State legislators. These men worked in three main industries, mining, agriculture and pastoralism. [396]

They first lived at Peri, in Finch Hatton and then Bakers Creek before settling on Northside (North Mackay) in 1908.[397] It was not possible to find where James Jung lived on the electoral roll possibly because he was not an Australian citizen. Peri Sugar Mill was erected on Peri Plantation in 1885 but was never operational. The plantation was owned by Thomas Fitzgerald's son who took over the property in 1873.[398]

The couple had twelve children although not all children survived to adulthood. Two of the children were registered with the surname of both Sam and Sampson (Amelia Edith and Charles James Sampson). Elizabeth Mary Sampson was only registered as having the surname Sampson. Their births were re-registered later with James Jung as the father, but the couple were not married at

---

[395] 'James Jung Sam', 2023, *Find a Grave*, viewed 18/10/2023 https://www.findagrave.com
[396] Robb, Sandi, 2019, *North Queensland's Chinese Family Landscape: 1860 - 1920*, Townsville, James Cook University.
[397] Mackay Family History Society, 2012, 'Mary Ann Sam', Mackay, The Society.
[398] Hall, Glen, 2003, 'Sugar Mills of the Mackay District', viewed 19-09-2023 http://www.mackayhistory.org/research/sugar_mills/peri.html

that time: Charles William Sam was born 1887 and died in 1948. He was also registered as Charles James Sampson, being born 16 January 1887. Anna (Annie) Beatrice Sam Moy was born 1888 and died 1972; Mary Elizabeth Sampson Joy was born in 1890 and died in 1927; Arthur (Arty) was born 1892 and died in 1990; Emily (Emma) Rebecca was born 1895; Walter James was born 1896 and died 1994; Amelia Edith was born 1899 and died in 1901; George Joseph was born 1901 and died in 1996; Frederick Henry was born 1904 and died in 1993; and Frances Albert was born 1906 and died in 1984.[399]

Arthur enlisted in the 12th Battalion, Australian Imperial Force, World War I and saw action in France. He was medically discharged in 1919 and lived until he was 98.[400] Mary Ann was also accredited with having reared Cecil George, Robert Samuel (Bob), William Thomas (Bill) and Henrietta (Hetty) Chung from childhood, all of whom regarded her as their mother.[401]

Mary Ann Sam was regarded as a hard worker for the community. Her nickname was the 'Grand Old lady of North Side'.[402] She raised funds at stalls, benefits and dances during World War I and assisted at Anzac Day lunches since inception. She was also a hard worker for the Northside Church of England. She volunteered her time for many benevolent and charitable events, extending kindness to all she met. She was known for her consideration towards others for which she was held in high esteem. As a mother, Sam supported her children at sporting events. Football, tennis and cricket were her main interests. She was an avid supporter of the Magpies team with whom all her sons played. She was a regular attendee at the

---

[399] Queensland Government, 1936, *Deaths in the District of Rockhampton, in the State of Queensland,* Rockhampton, The Government.

[400] National Archives Australia, 1919, 'Sam Arthur', viewed 31-10-2023 https://recordsearch.naa.go.au/SearchNRetrieve/Interface/ViewIn...

[401] Gcasandra, 2018, '10 Pioneering Women who Shaped Mackay's Future', *The Courier Mail,* viewed 2023-04-14 https://www.couriermail.com.au/news/queensland/mackay/ p.[10].

[402] ibid., p. [11].

Showgrounds for football events. Her hospitality was extended to include visiting football and cricket teams, coming from other cities and welcomed them into her home.[403] In recognition of her community work, the Queensland State Government Minister for Communities and Housing opened the *Mary Ann Sam*, a social housing complex in Palmer Street, of twenty-four new homes at North Mackay in 2021.[404]

The necessity for an eye operation meant that Sam went to Rockhampton in September 1936. It was in September 1936 that the births of their ten children were registered as being of Mary Ann Sam and James Sam on the same date as her marriage to James Sam - recorded on 12 September 1936, one month prior to her death in October. Just before her return to Mackay, she suffered a heart attack and died on 26 October. Her body was returned to Mackay, and she was buried in the Mackay Cemetery. Her obituary in the *Daily Mercury* stated that 'Not only North Side but the whole district is the poorer for her passing.'[405] She was 69 years old when she died. James Jung Sam lived to the age of 88 years.[406]

Events:

- 1884 Arrived at Rockhampton (Keppel Bay).
- 1908 First lived in North Mackay.

Links:

Watkins, Lillian, 2021, 'Mackay Social Housing Opens up on Palmer St in North Mackay', *The Courier Mail*, viewed 18/10/2023 https://www.couriermail.com.au...

---

[403] ibid., p. [11].
[404] Watkins, Lillian, 2021, 'Mackay Social Housing Opens Up On Palmer St in North Mackay', *The Courier Mail*, viewed 18/10/2023 https://www.couriermail.com.au
[405] 'Obituary Mrs J Sam', 1936, *Daily Mercury*, 28 October, p.9., viewed 18/10/2023, http://nla/gov/au/nla.news-article170252135
[406] 'Mary Ann Sam', 2023, *Find a Grave*, viewed 18/10/2023, https://www.findagrave.com

Figure 55 Mary Ann Sam and members of her family - Sam Family Collection – *Facebook*

Shuttlewood, Norma May, OAM (1925-2023)

Figure 56 Norma May Shuttlewood OAM 2023. Photograph courtesy of *ABC Tropical North*.

Born:
- 30 June 1925
- Home Hill, Queensland.

Died:
- 1 March 2023
- Mackay, Queensland.

Occupation:
- Musician, legal secretary and volunteer. Shuttlewood made an enormous contribution to music education in Mackay and district.

Alternative Name/s:
- Norma May Hague

Summary:

Norma May Hague was born at Home Hill, North Queensland. She was the second eldest daughter of Ethel May and William

Henry Hague. At the age of 10, her mother entered her in an Eisteddfod in the Burdekin. 'I sang a solo, played the violin, and I sang with the Home Hill school choir, and I really think that was where it all started.'[407] She learned the violin and piano at Home Hill and Ayr. Her education to year 10 was completed in Ayr when she finished Junior. She travelled to Mackay with her mother and younger sister seeking employment at the end of 1940. Her eldest sister Thelma was already working in Mackay. It was here that she gained employment as a legal secretary.[408]

At the age of 22, Hague was a competitor in the first eisteddfod held in Mackay following the end of the Second World War. She commented in an interview, 'There were only four sessions, just piano, singing, choral and there might have been highland dancing.'[409] She was awarded about two shillings and sixpence. Playing piano in the streets of Mackay at the end of the War was an experience. At the time, she worked for the law firm of Barron and Allen. She was enticed away from work to play the piano for eight hours on the back of a truck to celebrate the end of the war in 1945. Her daughter wrote in her eulogy that Hague said, 'I had blisters on all my fingers, but it was a great day.'[410]

The electoral records indicated that Hague was living at 54 Nelson Street prior to her marriage to Rodger Shuttlewood in St Patrick's Catholic Church, Mackay, on 18 April 1949.[411] Rodger was the

---

[407] Philpott, Meecham, and Harriet Tatham, 2016, '91 Year Old's Lifelong Love for the Stage Displayed in Unique Collection', *ABC Tropical North*, viewed 21-01-2024 https://www.abc.net.au/news/2016-10-04/91-year-old-eisteddfod-veteran-reflects-on-her-love-of-the-stage/7901234

[408] Shuttlewood, Kerry, 2024, *Interview*, telephone 1 March 2024.

[409] Devenport, Zoe, 2023, 'Norma Shuttlewood OAM Remembered as a Treasure and Icon of Mackay', *The Courier Mail*, viewed 03-01-2024 https://www.couriermail.com.au/news/queensland/mackay/community/norma-shuttlewood-oam-remembered-as-a-treasure-and-icon-of-mackay/news-story/124c0c09d3fc64725cb9164289df30df

[410] ibid.

[411] Queensland Government, Family History Research Service, 1949, *Marriage Registration*, viewed 27-02-2024 https://www.familyhistory.bdm.qld.gov.au/

eldest son of Ethel Mary Ford and Rodger Patrick Shuttlewood. He was born In Toowoomba on 9 November 1923 and attended Christian Brothers College in Bundaberg before gaining employment as a shoe salesman at Beirne's Ltd in Mackay. Surviving seven years in the Australian Army during World War II (1940-1947), he returned to work at Beirne's before he joined Queensland Rail in the mid-1970s as a fireman. He later became a qualified train driver. They had five children, Lesley Norma Shuttlewood Taylor, Jillian Frances Shuttlewood (10 October 1954-16 August 1976), Mark Rodger Shuttlewood, Jan Christine Shuttlewood Lawrence and Kerry Elizabeth Shuttlewood.[412]

After many years on stage, Shuttlewood joined the eisteddfod committee. 'In 1966 I took over as secretary for one week when the eisteddfod was in a bit of dire straits. Eighteen years later I resigned. In those days if people gave a donation, they had to have a receipt for the income tax, so I used to pedal my bike around town delivering receipts, she said.[413] In 1979 she was made a life member of the committee and Life Governor of the North Queensland Eisteddfod Council.

Shuttlewood was awarded Mackay's Australia Day Citizen of the Year award by Mayor Councillor Gordon White in 1997. The award was for outstanding community service on the eisteddfod committee, Mackay Child Minding Association, children's choirs, Mackay Table Tennis Association and Mackay Choral Society.[414] She was treasurer for twelve years for the Mackay Child Minding Association. Also, 'She started conducting children's school choirs in 1960 and at one time conducted 10 choirs at one eisteddfod.'[415]

Spanning a lifetime, her interests were wide and varied. She became a life member of the Mackay Choral Society, Mackay Eisteddfod Association, Mackay Table Tennis Association and

---

[412] Shuttlewood, Kerry, op. cit.
[413] ibid.
[414] 'Shuttlewood City Citizen of the Year', 1997, *The Daily Mercury*, January 27, p.3.
[415] ibid.

Life Governor of the North Queensland Eisteddfod Association. For these achievements she was awarded the Order of Australia Medal (OAM) in 1998 for services to the community especially for her work for the Mackay Eisteddfod Committee and the Catholic Women's League.[416]

Collecting memorabilia during her lifetime was a rewarding hobby. Shuttlewood stored the information in six binders and fourteen scrapbooks including every Mackay Eisteddfod program since 1947. Photographs were clipped from newspapers and pasted into scrapbooks.

> Whenever there was a photo in the paper it got cut out and put in a scrap book, Mrs Shuttlewood said. It's a lot of cutting and pasting, particularly at eisteddfod time, because mostly the Mercury [local paper] will put some photos in every day, so that keeps me very busy.[417]

Shuttlewood was described as an 'icon' and a 'treasure'. She was a working mother before it was a 'done thing' for married women to work. She had to take some flak for that at the time. She was also described as raising five talented and amazing children as well as contributing to the community.[418] She died at the age of 97 and was buried in the Mount Bassett Cemetery, Mackay.

Events:
- 1935 Burdekin Eisteddfod
- 1945 Mackay Eisteddfod
- 1966 Secretary of Mackay Eisteddfod Committee
- 1979 Life Member of the Mackay Eisteddfod Committee
- 1997 Mackay's Australia Day Citizen of the Year.
- 1998 Order of Australia (OAM) presented.

---

[416] Devenport, Zoe, op. cit.
[417] Philpott, Meecham and Harriet Tatham, op. cit.
[418] Davenport, Zoe, op. cit.

Awards:

The Norma Shuttlewood O A M Bursary:

In each art form the local competitor/s (15 to 25 years) who, in the opinion of the Adjudicator present/s the most outstanding performance, will receive $200. Candidates are to be chosen from Solo, Duo, Trio and Quartet sections.

Struthers, Mary Ellen (Min) (1903-1988)

**Figure 57 Min Struthers.
Photograph courtesy of Mackay Family History Society**

Born:
- 18 September 1903
- Toowoomba Queensland

Died:
- 3 December 1988
- Brisbane, Queensland

Occupation:
- Alderman Mackay City Council, member of the Mackay Regional Electricity Board and founder of Mackay Meals on Wheels. Struthers made a major contribution to social life of Mackay and district residents.

Alternative Name/s:
- Mary Ellen (Minnie) Fox

Summary:

Mary Ellen (Minnie) Fox was born in 1903 in Toowoomba, Queensland, the eldest child of William and Mary Fox (nee Collins). She had two brothers and two sisters. She was educated at St. Saviours School Toowoomba, and later married Robert (Bob) Struthers 29 October 1937 in Toowoomba and moved to Boonah where Bob was employed by the Education Department. Bob was later transferred to Proserpine in 1941. They had one daughter, Ruth Struthers Clark.

The Struthers family started their furniture business in Proserpine with Bob building large wooden toys. The couple devoted themselves to raising money for the war effort with community concerts, balls and other social events. They developed their toy making business to incorporate household furniture, made by hand. It was in 1946 that they moved to Mackay, and established a very successful business, Struthers Furniture. Bob Struthers & Company displayed furniture and pianos at the Mackay Show in 1949[419] and purchased a new building in Mackay City costing between $15,000 and $20,000 in 1951 to build a new furniture emporium with an attached funeral parlour.[420] Their daughter, Ruth Clark commented that her parents had managed the store in Mackay from 1943 to 1967, when she and her husband John managed the store until it was sold in the 1980s.[421]

In 1967, Struthers campaigned as an independent and was elected to Mackay City Council, (in April 1967, re-elected in April 1970 and March 1973) becoming the second woman to serve on the Council. The first woman to be elected to the Mackay City Council was Miss Mary Finlay in 1937. Shruthers was the first woman to serve on the Mackay Regional Electricity Board (1967-1973).[422]

---

[419] 'Luxury Lines in Furniture', 1949, *Daily Mercury*, Monday 27 June, p.8., viewed 2023-01-19 https://nla.gov.au/
[420] 'New $15,000 City Building', 1951, *Daily Mercury*, Thursday 6 September, p.2. viewed 2023-01-19 https://nla.gov.au
[421] ibid.
[422] 'Former Mackay Alderman Dies', 1988, *Daily Mercury*, 6 December, p.7.

She later became the president of the Australian Women's Local Government Association and was a member of many local organisations. Renowned for her forthright comments and debates, she was also kind, honest and forward thinking. Struthers would see a project through from beginning to end with a fervour which was formidable. Her campaign for seats in the city streets was an example of her tenacity when she was 'on a mission.'[423]

It was in 1967 that Struthers founded Mackay Meals on Wheels. She was awarded life-time membership and became a patron of Meals on Wheels (MOW). To raise money for MOW, she tirelessly campaigned for donations from all sources that included roaming the show grounds on day three of the Mackay Show asking for a contribution.

When she retired from the Council for health reasons, her parting words were: 'I have enjoyed working for Mackay and its citizens. It has been a turbulent but exciting nine years, and I can only hope that without me they will not die of boredom.'[424]

Her special interests were golf, contract bridge, entertaining, gardening and reading. Min Struthers died in Brisbane on 3 December 1988.

Events:

- 1946 Arrived in Mackay and established Struthers Furniture
- 1967 Elected to Mackay City Council
- 1967 Elected first female to the Mackay Regional Electricity Board
- 1967 Founded Mackay Meals on Wheels.

---

[423] Mackay Family History Society, 2012, 'Min Struthers', Mackay, The Society.
[424] ibid.

Tanner, Eliza Jane (1866-1935)

Figure 58 Eliza Tanner. Photograph courtesy Nita Patterson.

Born:
- 28 January 1866
- Spring Hill, Brisbane, Queensland.

Died:
- 10 June 1935
- Cromer Hospital, Shakespeare Street, Mackay, Queensland.

Occupation:
- Country Women's Association (CWA), committee member, Mackay Branch and Life member and President of the Women's Auxiliary Committee of the District Hospital. Foundation member of the Ladies Anzac Day Luncheon Committee, and during World War I, Committee member Red Cross League Branch. Tanner was an industrious and dedicated member of Mackay society.

Alternative Name/s:
- Eliza Jane Harrison, Eliza Jane Gutteridge

Summary:

Eliza Jane was the only daughter amongst six brothers of Samuel Harrison, an engineer, and Mary Ann Wells who was born in County Kent, England. Wells arrived in Australia aboard the vessel *Whirlwind* in 1862. Formerly a Gympie resident where her family were amongst the earliest of residents, Eliza Jane Harrison married George Gutteridge at the age of 19 on 13 August 1885 at St Paul's Anglican Church, Ipswich. George was born in Rushworth Victoria in 1861. He was a skilled wheelwright and carriage builder who was amongst the first in Mackay to build carriage wheels wholly completed.[425] Census records indicate that her husband George worked at Walkerston about 11 km from Mackay.

The couple had ten children. Those children were: Charles Lionel Gutteridge (1885-1933); Elaine violet Gutteridge (1887-1925); Ivy Gutteridge (1889-1899); Edith (Edie) Lillian Gutteridge Bonfield Hamilton (1893-1980); Walter Ernest Gutteridge (1897-1897); William (Bill) Joseph Gutteridge (1898-1971); Alma Myrtle Gutteridge Poulton (1902-1992); Samuel Arthur (Artie) Gutteridge (1905-1985); Hilda Veronica Gutteridge (1907-1908) and the youngest son, Artie, was born at the family home in 32 Wellington Street, Mackay.[426]

Gutteridge was the sole owner of this property which she purchased in 1904. Along with the home, she also purchased an adjoining allotment to the rear, that faced Albert Street, (now Gordon Street), Mackay. Before relocating to Mackay, Gutteridge made several trips by sea often with the children to

---

[425] 'Obituary Mrs Eliza Tanner', 1935, *Daily Mercury*, Wednesday 12 June, p.9. viewed 20/08/2024 http://trove.nla.gov.au
[426] Patterson, Nita, 2021, 'Eliza Jane Gutteridge Formerly Harrison', Mackay, The Author, p.1.

spend time with George. These were the days when sea transport was prevalent because rail or road transport was either not built or unreliable.

Gutteridge was an independent, community focused woman who enjoyed working for several charitable organisations. She was one of the earliest Committee Members of the Mackay Branch of the Country Women's Association (CWA), a life member of the Women's Auxiliary Committee of the District Hospital. One of her roles was that of president. Gutteridge gained special recognition of hospital Committee and Staff for her work providing comfort and cheer to patients. She was also a foundation member of the Ladies Anzac Day Luncheon Committee. During World War I, she was an untiring worker for men in service.[427] When the Red Cross League branch was first formed in August 1914, Gutteridge was a committee member. Her granddaughter regarded her as …'a charitable and talented lady, skilled in many crafts and her handicraft was greatly admired.' Gutteridge owned and held a driver's license for her T Model Ford.[428]

Following the death of her husband George in 1930, Eliza married Walter Tanner, a farmer of Balnagowan on 22 November 1932. She died three years later at the age of 69 years and was buried in the Mackay City Cemetery. In the last year of her life, her health gradually declined. She was reluctantly forced to relinquish prominent positions held by her on many semi-public organisations. In her last month of life, she was confined to her bed and died.[429] Walter Tanner, her second husband subdivided the land and sold off two sections but kept the house. Two sons of George and Eliza reside in the Mackay district and recently the birth of a fifth generation of the Gutteridge family was celebrated.

---

[427] 'Mackay Notes', 1935, *Townsville Bulletin*, 25 June, p.9. viewed 22/08/2024 http://nla/gov/au/nla.news-article61979920

[428] Patterson, Nita, op. cit.

[429] Obituary, op.cit.

Events:

- 1904 Purchased a house and land at 32 Wellington Street, Mackay.
- 1905 Women's Auxiliary Committee of the Mackay District Hospital.[430]
- 1914 Volunteer for World War I causes.
- 1923 CWA began in Mackay.

Figure 59 The Gutteridge family home at 32 Wellington Street, Mackay. Photograph courtesy of Nita Patterson.

---

[430] 'Helping the Hospital', 1906, *Daily Mercury*, Friday 2 February, p.2. viewed 27/08/2024 http://http://nla.gov.au/nla.news-article171570308

Trieve, Rowena Evelyn OAM (1931-2018)

Figure 60 Rowena Trieve OAM. Photograph courtesy of *The Courier Mail*.

Born:
- 22 February 1931
- Mackay, Queensland

Died:
- 6 September 2018
- Mackay, Queensland

Occupation:
- Elder, Australian South Sea Islander (ASSI) community, laundry supervisor, Order of Australia recipient in 2003, a fashion designer and business woman. Trieve was a former president of the ASSI Association and recognised as a Multicultural Ambassador (Regional) in 2013. She made a significant contribution not only to her community of Islanders but also to the wider Australian community.

Alternative Name/s:
- Rowena Evelyn Thomas, Aunty Rowena Trieve.

Summary:

Rowena Thomas was a daughter of William (Bill) Thomas and Irene Ivy Marlla Thomas. She had a brother Bill Jnr and a sister Irene. Rowena was the granddaughter of Katie Marlla, thought to be the inspiration for her achievements, and a second cousin of Gloria Arrow. On her paternal side of the family her grandmother was of Aboriginal and Sri Lankan heritage. Her father, Bill, reportedly taught himself to read and ensured his children had a good education. As an adult, her brother became a Deputy Principal of a school.[431] Thomas attended Homebush State School and worked for a time at Eungella Station as a domestic in 1958, and as a laundry worker for more than thirty years. She married Kevin Joseph Trieve with whom she had two sons. In her later years, as well as working, and caring for her family, and her community work, she cared for her aging parents.

Trieve actively promoted the interests of the ASSI community particularly in the Mackay region. A Commonwealth Government grant was made by the Member for Dawson, De-Anne Kelly, to Rowena Trieve and Jeanette Morgan that financially contributed to the creation of their designer label, Famouri.[432]

Trieve also played a significant role in the ASSI community as a volunteer. She held the volunteer roles of president, secretary and treasurer of the Mackay & District Australian South Sea Islander Association (MADASSIA) and the ASSI community. It is believed that one of her major legacies was, with the assistance of Sue Waite, the development of the Protocols Document. This document provided guidelines for government bodies and people in general who would like to work within the ASSI community. Her work has

---

[431] Kelly, De-Anne, 2000, Canberra, *Commonwealth of Australia, Parliamentary Debates*, Monday 28 August, viewed 20/08/2023, http://parlinfo.aph.gov.au
[432] ibid.

given recognition of the ASSI's culture and place in Queensland's history where the largest numbers of the community live today.[433]

Treive was awarded the Order of Australia in 2003 for her service to the ASSI community. It was in 2008 that a block of housing units was named in her honour at Bridge Road Mackay. The then Housing Minister Robert Schwarten, was in Mackay for the Bligh Government's community Cabinet. He was joined by the Member for Mackay Tim Mulherin who named the complex, Rowena Trieve Place. He mentioned that Trieve was a third-generation descendant of a Pacific Islander and had lived in Mackay all her life. 'She has devoted her life to improvements for Australian South Sea Islanders and in building bridges to the wider community, he said.'[434] She was commended for her contribution to implementation of the Recognition Statements across three levels of government.[435]

In 2013, Trieve was awarded the title of Multicultural Ambassador (Regional) for the Mackay region in recognition for her voluntary service to the Australian South Sea Islander community. Her work involved assisting the community to connect with their heritage by engaging cultural tutors from the Solomon Islands and Vanuatu to conduct cultural workshops for the community.[436]

She also teamed up with Mal Meninga, a Queensland State of Origin legend, whose antecedents were also from the South Sea Islands, to increase community awareness. They jointly developed a university scholarship program for young people. Many of the government committees and working parties she served on included social justice issues such as women's issues, antiracism, heritage, training, home and community care.[437]

---

[433] *Sweet Anarchy*, 2023, viewed 21/8/2023, http://www.sweetanarchy.com.au/stability.html
[434] ibid.
[435] Queensland Government, 2008, 'New Social Housing Dwelling Named after Mackay Great', viewed 23/08/2023, https://statements.qld.gov.au/statements/53354
[436] Queensland Government, 2013, 'Award recipient: Mrs Rowena Trieve OAM', viewed 21/08/2023, https://www.qld.gov.au/about/events-awards-honours/awards/multicultural-queensland-awards/past-winners/2013-winners
[437] *Courier Mail*, 2018, 'An Inspiration to Her Community', September 29, viewed 6/09/2023, https://www.newsbank.com/libraries/international/access-global-newsbank-2023-edition

Trieve has been described as a courageous and formidable woman, and a gentle leader who was much loved and who inspired her community. Her motto was 'you can't change your history, but you can make sure it wasn't in vain.'[438] She left two sons, three grandchildren and a great granddaughter, her husband having predeceased her in 2009. She was buried in Walkerston Cemetery near Mackay, Queensland.

Events:
- 2008 Rowena Trieve Place

Awards:
- 2003 Order of Australia
- 2013 Multicultural Ambassador (Regional)

Links:

Rowena Trieve Place: https://statements.qld.gov.au/statements/53354

**Figure 61 Rowena Trieve OAM 2013.
Photograph courtesy of Archetype Imaging.**

---

[438] ibid.

Wallman, Marilyn Joy (1958-1972)

Figure 62 Marilyn Wallman. Photograph courtesy of *The Daily Mercury*.

Born:
- 6 March 1958
- Mackay, Queensland

Died:
- 21 March 1972
- Mackay, Queensland

Occupation/Event:
- Student who was kidnapped and murdered. Her loss impacted the local and wider Australian community. Following this event, people were made more aware of the need to closely supervise their children's travel to school and away from home.

Alternative name/s:
- Marilyn Wallman

Summary:

Marilyn Joy Wallman was 14 years old when she disappeared. She was riding her push-bike down a country lane at 7.42 am to the bus stop prior to boarding the school bus to high school at 8 am, when she disappeared in a dip in the road unseen from the family home. Her two younger brothers David aged 11, and Rex aged 9, were following, 10 minutes behind. Her bike was found lying on the road, its front wheel still spinning. Her schoolbag (port) and contents were scattered, and her school hat had landed amongst the six-feet tall stands of sugar cane beside the road. David rushed home to alert his mother while Rex guarded her bike and belongings. It was then that he thought he heard his sister saying that her legs were hurting.[439]

Daphne Joyce and John William Wallman had three children prior to their eldest daughter's disappearance. A daughter Lenore was born after the two boys. The family began a search for Marilyn. John Wallman was away fishing that day and joined the search later in the afternoon. The police were not called until later that day. It became one of the largest search parties in the history of the Mackay district. Police in large numbers and more than 300 volunteers conducted shoulder to shoulder searches of the surrounding cane fields and bush in the vicinity of the abduction. More than 160 km of highways, roads and tracks were searched - some on horseback. Numerous creeks, gullies and bridges were searched on the advice of two clairvoyants.[440]

The police identified three vehicles of interest with two owners being discounted as being involved. The third car was never found

---

[439] Kyriacou, Kate, 2014, 'The Brother of a Girl Missing Since 1972 Still Searches for Answers', *The Courier Mail*, 13 December, viewed 4/01/2021 https://www.couriermail.com.au/news/queensland/the-girl-of-missing-since-1972-still-searches-for-answers/news-

[440] Wright, Richie, 2018, *Marilyn Joy Wallman (195801972: Find a Grave Memorial*, viewed 5 March 2024 https://www.findagrave.com/memorial/18977077/marilyn-joy-wallman...

or identified. Several persons of interest have been identified over the years although no one has been formally charged. After six days police determined that Marilyn had been abducted and murdered by person or persons unknown in a place and by methods unknown. Fragments of Wallman's skull were found by one of the persons of interest, Greven Breadsell of Mirani West in 1974. These bone fragments were found 40 km from where she disappeared. They were extensively tested by police in Australia, the United States of America and New Zealand and finally identified by DNA testing. The bond fragments were identified as belonging to Marilyn Wallman.[441]

Wallman's sugar cane farm at Eimeo was in a remote, isolated area in 1972. Eimeo is a coastal town and suburb of Mackay about 10 to 15 minutes' drive from the city centre. The name Eimeo was derived from a pastoral run name used by Jeremiah Downs Armitage, a pastoralist in the 1870s, possibly because of his birthplace in Tahiti, claimed to be Moorea (also called Eimeo). Eimeo Road State School opened on 5 February 1934. It was the largest primary school in the Whitsunday region, Mackay region, and Isaac region. It is no longer within the boundaries of Eimeo but within the neighbouring suburb of Rural View. Wallman and her two brothers went to the Eimeo Road State School, only a few minutes bike ride from their home, prior to her attending high school.

Mackay and Eimeo were places where everyone knew everyone else. It was not possible to do or say much at all that everyone did not know about or comment on. Wright commented, 'Mackay was a much smaller place where most people knew one another. It was a vibrant town in 1972. The sugar industry was doing very well right up through that era.'[442] The township

---

[441] Lcommerford and Ekert, Janessa, 2015, 'Bone Fragment Released to Marilyn Wallman's Family, *The Courier Mail*, viewed 3/05/2023 https://www.couriermail.com.au/news/queensland/mackay/bone-fragment-released-to-marilyn-wallmans-family/news-story/384b2893c2b47ad9517d30254f239322
[442] ibid., p.1.

as it was then developed on the southern bank of the Pioneer River through to the city gates. The rest of it was on the north side which belonged to the Pioneer Shire Council. Mackay's population both urban and rural was around 59,000 people at that time.[443]

Reporters commented that when Wallman disappeared, the community was initially slow to react. 'What was amazing was that initially there was a search that did not include the police. It probably wasn't taken seriously at first.' The family and neighbours conducted the search around the area and then it was decided to call the police. 'Nowadays if something like that happened the police would be there immediately.'[444]

The impact of Wallman's disappearance and murder changed the lives of her family, friends, the local and wider Australian community. 'There has never been a community affected by a murder quite like how Mackay was shaken and shaped by Marilyn Wallman's disappearance.'[445] That was the finding by Monash University's Belinda Morrissey. The communications and writing lecturer, who specialises in disappearances and trauma, studied Wallman's case when she co-authored an article about a small community's reaction to the teenager's disappearance. 'There have been similar cases in tiny communities, but it doesn't seem to have the same impact," she said. 'This really shaped Mackay.'[446]

Morrissey said the fact that Wallman went missing in a remote and isolated area added to the community's fear. 'Initially they wanted to help. About 300 people looked for Marilyn, on foot,

---

[443] *Commonwealth Census* 1971
[444] Hegarty, Laura and Meecham Philpot, 2014, 'How Marilyn Wallman's Disappearance Changed Mackay', *ABC Local*, 11 February, viewed 13/01/2021 https://www.abc.net.au
[445] Davy, A., 2014, 'Marilyn Wallman's Disappearance Really Shaped Mackay,' *Daily Mercury*, 8 February, viewed 2/02/2021 http://www.dailymercury.com.au
[446] ibid.

in four-wheel drives and even on horses. Her disappearance also frightened parents. Mothers started driving their kids to school instead of letting them walk or ride bikes.'[447]

The impact on her brothers and parents also changed their lives. Rex Wallman, because of the trauma of losing Wallman, suffered throughout his life the fear of losing a loved one. He describes an incident when he went to collect his son who was being minded by a baby-sitter while his wife was at work. The baby-sitter was late by half an hour returning home to her house with the child. He had been on the phone telephoning people to find out why the sitter was not home. 'About half an hour later, she pulls into the driveway. She'd decided to take them down to the beach for a while. So, you know, I lost it and grabbed Julian. He wasn't going back there again. Just about the whole night I sat in his room, either holding him or sitting beside this cot. I just could not make that lady understand.'[448]

Daphne Wallman commented that both her sons had suffered emotional stress throughout their lives. 'Both boys had breakdowns. It gets to them. The police gave Rex a terrible gruelling, 'Are you sure you are not telling lies? – about what you heard in the cane. It was the worst thing they ever did to him. It haunts him. It's the cause of a lot of his problems today.'[449]

The aftermath of the disappearance of Marilyn not only had consequences for her family but across generations and much more widely than just the local area which has had a lasting effect. Parents across Australia seldom allowed their children to walk or ride to school following the disappearance of Marilyn Wallman. Her funeral was held in 2015, forty-two years after her disappearance on what would have been Wallman's 57th birthday.

---

[447] ibid.
[448] Morrissey, Belinda and Davis, Kristen, 'Dead Ends: The Vanishing of Marilyn Wallman', viewed 20/02/2024 http://researchonline.federation.edu.au/vital/access/HandleResolver/1959.17/190369 p.171.
[449] ibid.

Jonathan Hair, a journalist, reported that there was more than 300 people who turned out for the funeral in Mackay, many wearing yellow, her favourite colour.[450] Yellow was often included in the clothes made by her mother. Her brother Rex said the funeral would give people closure and the family would now have a grave to visit. 'We now will have somewhere we can go; you know, we're going to be able to go to Marilyn's plot and sit on the grass and have a talk to her ... and know that she's actually there now, Rex said.' [451]

'A kiss and a smile then she vanished forever'. That's the inscription on Marilyn Joy Wallman's headstone. Marilyn, just 14, gave her mother a kiss and her easy smile then cycled away from home, vanishing out of their lives. She was ...'laid to rest beneath the eucalypts at Mount Basset, a typical Mackay environment with its familiar bush smells and sounds, for all who knew her, or who learned about the bubbly schoolgirl, it is a site where they pray, she truly finds peace.'[452]

Events:

- 1972 Abduction and death.
- 1974 Skull fragments found and identified.
- 2015 Funeral service and burial of remains interred at Mount Bassett Cemetery, Mackay.

Links:

A plaque was laid at Marilyn Wallman Park. A tree was planted in her honour: https://monumentaustralia.org.au/themes/people/crime/display/107990-marilyn-wallman

---

[450] Hair, Jonathan, 2015, *Daily Mercury*, viewed 12/01/2021, https://www.abc.net.au/news/2015-03-06/marilyn-wallman-funeral-held-in-mackay/6286400
[451] ibid.
[452] ibid.

Figure 63 David, Rex, Lenore, John, and Daphne Wallman in 2022. Photograph courtesy of *The Courier Mail*.

Wood, Hilma Pansy, Miss (1903-1984)

Figure 64 Miss Hilma Pansy Wood. Photograph courtesy of the *Daily Mercury*.

Born:
- 2 February 1903
- Mackay, Queensland.

Died:
- 30 April 1984
- Mackay, Queensland.

Occupation:
- Musician, Artist and Photographer. Wood dedicated her life to teaching music and made an enormous contribution to the music community in Mackay.

Alternative Name/s:
- Pansy Wood, 'Woody'.

Summary:

Pansy Wood as she was known, was the daughter of John Wood and Annie Christie. Her brother, Ian Alexander Christie Wood, was a well-known travel agent and former Senator. Neither of the siblings married.

Her music career began somewhat accidently when her mother purchased a raffle ticket in aid of the district hospital from a family friend. The prize was a second hand piano. The Wood family won a French made Aucher Freres piano (circa 1880-1920), made by the Aucher Brothers of Paris. Wood studied music with Mrs Mowbray Campbell, and then under Miss Blanche Gralow, who later became Mrs Cecil Shephard. Under Miss Gralow's tutelage, she gained her first real appreciation for music and an Associate Diploma of Trinity College, London (ATCL).[453]

At the age of 14, she was giving lessons to students while a student herself. Her brother Ian was working as an office junior clerk earning ten shillings a week therefore, he could afford to pay for her lessons at ten shillings per quarter. Her mother was '… passionately fond of music although she had only learned a little herself in Scotland.'[454]

Wood later became more ambitious and coached herself for the Licentiate Performer's Diploma (LAB) of the Royal School of Music, London. Ian Wood commented that in her prime, Pansy '…had been a very fine musician. She once tied for second place at the Rockhampton Eisteddfod with a student Jack Villaume, who became a musical celebrity in Queensland.'[455]

Following the Rockhampton Eisteddfod experience, the adjudicator, Sydney May, who was an examiner for the Australian board of Music wrote to her and expressed interest in her career.

---

[453] 'Music Teacher Dies at 81', 1984, *Daily Mercury*, 1 May, p.6.
[454] ibid.
[455] 'Music Teacher Dies at 81', op. cit.

"He went to the trouble of writing a book on music by hand (including the music itself) because it was out of print, and he said he wanted me to have it."[456]

Wood contributed to many musical events in Mackay. She played for the Mackay Choral Society as a solo pianist at choir concerts, and she was the first pianist to be engaged by ABC Radio when the Mackay studio was first established, accompanying artists performing over the air waves. Other events at which she regularly played during the thirties and forties included the Presbyterian Church musical exhibitions and the Gibb's Variety Show which consisted of dancing, singing and ballet performances.[457]

Multi-talented, Wood displayed drawing skills with charcoal and photography for which she took lessons from the Mackay Camera Group. The charcoal drawings took the form of portraits which adorned her living room walls. Her work was acknowledged at many of the Mackay shows.

Music was her first love in life, even though she could be regarded as a strict teacher, the outcome of her talents was represented in the achievements of her many students. Mavis Braithwaite (nee Rigbye) passed the Associate Diploma (AmusA) for musical performance and musical theory at the age of 14 years and holds the record for the youngest Mackay student to achieve that.[458]

Rigbye began her musical career with piano lessons at the age of five at Pansy Wood's Music Centre in Peel Street, Mackay.[459]

---

[456] '60 Years Spent as Mackay Music Teacher', 1982, *Daily Mercury*, 11 August, p.17.
[457] ibid.
[458] ibid.
[459] At the age of 14 Mavis was recognised as the youngest person in Mackay to pass her A.Mus.A. with the Australian Music Examination Board. By the age of 16 she was an Associate of the Trinity College of London (ATCL) in performance and gained her. Licentiate (LTCL) in October 1955. In October 1957, Mavis was the only one of 11 entrants in Queensland to pass her Licentiate with the AMEB - L.Mus A. viewed 13/03/2024 https://mackaycommunityfoundation.com

Another student, Carolyn Lind (nee Wilson) became an excellent duettist with her music partner Lesley Horan, Pansy Wood recalled. 'They have won the grand champion duet two years in succession at the Mackay Eisteddfod.'[460] A successful pianoforte teacher trained by Wood was Pam Jensen, as Wood recalled. 'I find there are very few pupils who do not have some music in them', [and] I enjoy bringing it out.'[461]

Jensen said that she owed a lot to Pansy Wood and would not be where she was today had she not been able to call on her for guidance. Jensen was quoted as saying about Pansy Wood, 'She was a hard-working dedicated teacher who really loved her profession. She always spoke her mind, she added, and was the most honest person I knew.'[462] Pansy Wood died in 1984 aged 81 and was buried in Mt Bassett Cemetery, Mackay.

Events:

- 1992 The Pansy Wood Music Centre was established at the Whitsunday Anglican school by former Senator Ian Wood.

Awards:

Mackay Eisteddfod: Miss Pansy Wood Memorial Trophy - to be awarded to the local competitor competing in and securing the most points in all the following sections: – Grand Pianoforte Championship Solo, Solo by an Australian Composer Open, Bach Prelude and Fugue Open and Sonata Movement Solo Open. This is a perpetual trophy to be competed for annually and a replica will be presented as a memento.

---

[460] '60 Years Spent as Mackay Music Teacher', 1982, op. cit.
[461] ibid.
[462] 'Music Teacher Dies at 81', 1984 op. cit.

www.ingramcontent.com/pod-product-compliance
Lightning Source LLC
Chambersburg PA
CBHW061218070526
44584CB00029B/3880